An Undying Testimony

Keeping My Second Estate

KEELA JACKSON

authorHOUSE®

AuthorHouse™
1663 Liberty Drive
Bloomington, IN 47403
www.authorhouse.com
Phone: 1 (800) 839-8640

Published by AuthorHouse 05/26/2016

ISBN: 978-1-5246-0654-1 (sc)
ISBN: 978-1-5246-0652-7 (hc)
ISBN: 978-1-5246-0653-4 (e)

Library of Congress Control Number: 2016907132

Print information available on the last page.

Any people depicted in stock imagery provided by Thinkstock are models, and such images are being used for illustrative purposes only. Certain stock imagery © Thinkstock.

This book is printed on acid-free paper.

KJV - King James Version
The Book of Mormon -Another Testament of Christ

Scripture taken from the King James Version of the Bible and The Book of Mormon, Another Testament of Christ.

TABLE OF CONTENTS

DEDICATION

This book is dedicated to
Torcellous Jr., Andrew, Brianna, Sariah,
Aniyah, Na'Staljah, and Dakota,
who are my handsome nephews and beautiful
nieces. I love you with all my heart.
I have tried to find opportunities to teach
what I know to be true about life
and our Heavenly Father. This is just another way to testify that
God is real and knows us, and has a divine plan for each of us.

INTRODUCTION

This is my story of miracles witnessed and life lessons learned from going through the different experiences of having Systemic Lupus Erythematosus (SLE), also known as Lupus. It hasn't always been easy, but knowing and having the truth about God and His plan for my life has made it all worth it and endurable! Even in the midst of trials of pain and heartache you can still have the peace and joy that only comes from a divine power, the Lord Jesus Christ who loves us so much. You will see as I share experiences, sensitive feelings, and thoughts from my journal over the years how we can mature spiritually and grow close to the Lord when we allow Him to lead us.

"The windows of heaven are open wide to the faithful and righteous; nothing closes them faster than disobedience ... Diligent, enduring obedience to God's laws is the key that opens the windows of heaven. Obedience enables us to be receptive to the mind and will of the Lord. 'The Lord requireth the heart and a willing mind ..." (Joseph B. Wirthlin of the Quorum of the Twelve Apostles; Ensign, Nov. 1995, 75-76)

Chapter 1

HOW I GAINED MY TESTIMONY OF JESUS CHRIST

When I was a little girl, I was surrounded by many beautiful women whom I admired and wanted to become similar to. It wasn't so much the beauty that I admired, but their independence, their self-respect, and the influence that they had on the people around them. I just thought that these were powerful women in their own unique ways, and I wanted to be like that.

I wanted to become a woman who had a positive influence on young women and older women alike; I wanted to help them see their individual worth. Yet, this was just a want, and I never thought I could ever become like these women and the person I hoped to be. My life as a youth made my future seem so far away, as well as my hopes and dreams.

I grew up in the city of Chicago, in the home that my grandmother worked so hard to keep as a safe haven for her family. It was a good place to call home for a long time. It was a fun place to be, as we had all the company and entertainment a child could want. It was a two-story duplex that seemed liked a mansion to a child during relaxed time and a treasure box during playtime—though it felt too big of a place when it came to cleaning time. Six out of eight of my grandmother's children lived there with their children. There was never a boring moment in our home—or in our neighborhood, for that matter. Cousins were like brothers and sisters, and aunts and uncles were Mom and Dad when Mom and Dad weren't there. There was much love in that home for a time. Then things rapidly changed as the evilness of the world made its way into our home; destroying trust, peace, and family unity. Trials and tribulations were something that I became familiar with at a young age. "Growing up too fast" isn't the phrase that I would use for myself. It was more like learning how to survive at a young age. Knowing who to lie to, who to tell the truth to, who to take from, who to run from, who to turn to, who to keep from, how to manipulate, how to hustle, and how to survive in pure darkness, literally. There were times that I had nothing to eat, no hot water, maybe not even running water at all. Life became hard and unwanted for a ten-year-old girl who just wanted peace and to become someone who could make a difference in this world someday. I wanted out, and I wanted out fast. Yet, I loved my family, and I wanted to see them do better.

There was a time when I had to decide if I wanted to stay in Chicago with my mom, who wasn't able to care for me and my brother at the time, or move to Kentucky with close family members. I had never lived outside of Chicago or away from my mom or siblings for a long period of time. This was a hard decision to make, but I knew I had to do something if I ever wanted any hope for a better life. I prayed and was guided by God to go where He planned for me to go.

I do believe that God places certain people in your life at certain times for certain reasons. All my life, though I didn't know it at the time, I had the Lord guiding me through these trials and placing me around certain people to help build a foundation of faith, character, and an undying testimony. It started with the women whom I admired— my grandmother, my aunts, and my cousin Erica. As I matured and accepted the Gospel of Jesus Christ in my life, there were more people I was surrounded by who helped me build a solid testimony of who I am, what I'm capable of, and who I wanted to become.

My grandma always had a Holy Bible displayed somewhere in the house, opened up, inviting one to read. Usually I would see it in the cleanest room in the house on top of a white stand that looked like an old-fashioned record player or some type of entertainment center that no one ever touched. So I knew of the Bible, but I wasn't familiar with what was in it, not until later in my life.

Easter for us kids in the house and the neighborhood meant dressing up in our finest, collecting candy, and eating boiled eggs. That was all there was to it for most of us, and that was enough, so I thought. Then there was one Easter Sunday that was different for me. Something happened that made me hunger for more than just pretty dresses and candy. This particular Easter changed my view of life forever.

I can't remember how old I must have been—maybe ten or eleven years old, maybe younger. I can't remember exactly; however, I can remember being excited to put on my white tights, brand-new Easter dress, and new shoes. Getting new clothes was always exciting. I remember my pretty yellow dress with black flowers printed all over it, and the shoes were black and shiny with a little heel on them. I felt mature and sophisticated in my outfit. That's all I can remember about that day until later that evening, when it was time for the kids to go to bed.

Grandma had four bedrooms upstairs. The girl cousins always slept upstairs. This Easter night I was going to sleep in my grandma's room, which was the room right outside the living room, where everyone watched TV. I remember Auntie Lisa sitting on the floor in front of the floor-model television watching a movie. I was heading to the room, but then what was being shown on TV caught my attention. My auntie was narrating the movie. (I hate when people talk through the movie, but I was so glad that she was doing it at the time.)

The Greatest Story Ever Told was showing. Now, I knew nothing about this at the time, and that's why it caught my attention because I was shocked by what was happening and how it made me feel when I saw it. There was a man, half-naked, bloody, carrying a cross on His back while people were screaming at Him, spitting on Him, and being mean to Him. It broke my heart and I asked, "Why are they doing that to Him?" I remember my aunt trying to tell me what was happening. She told me that it was Jesus. Well, I knew of the name because people would say it all the time, mostly misusing it, but I didn't know anything more than that He was a man spoken of in the Bible. My mom was yelling at me from another room, telling me to go to bed. I had to watch a little more. I was in awe and wanted to see what happened. After I watched them nail His hands to the cross, I couldn't help but feel an overwhelming love for this Jesus. Why would they do that? I was more amazed at how He didn't fight back and didn't do anything to encourage the crowd to do what they were doing to Him. I needed to know more. I wanted to know more about Jesus. I knew that He was someone special, and I just had to learn about Him.

After that day, I begin to read the Holy Bible, even the one Grandma kept open for people to read. I wanted to know more about Jesus Christ. I read it constantly, starting in the New Testament, and I remember feeling good every time I would read it. My love for the Savior only grew stronger as I learned about Him and the many miracles He performed. One of my favorite Scripture stories that I loved reading about was the woman with the issue of blood. At the time I had no idea how much I had in common with this woman, and maybe that's why I loved her story so much, but it helped my testimony and faith.

I read about how, for many years, she'd tried to find ways to be healed from this disease that she had, but no one could help her. She'd tried everything, but still nothing or no one could help her. Then when she learned about Jesus Christ and how He was performing miracles, she thought to herself that if only she could touch the hem of His garment, she knew she'd be made whole. She didn't think it; she knew it. The Scriptures don't mention her having any other encounter with Jesus before this, only that she'd heard about Him performing miracles. Now, either her faith was exceedingly strong, or she just felt like she'd take a chance to see what happened. I think it was the first. She knew Jesus was special, heavenly, and powerful, and knew that she didn't have to talk with Him. She didn't even have to touch His flesh—just the hem of His garment—and she knew she'd be healed. What great faith! What great faith! So that is what she did, and in the midst of the crowd, the Lord felt the power escape Him.

Wow … something happened! Something happened that was between Him and the woman. Something personal, something sacred and powerful, and no one knew of it but the Lord and the woman. A relationship changed right then and there. As the Lord asked who it was who touched Him, I'm quite sure He knew who it was, but it was an experience for her and those around them. As she admitted to it being her, the Lord told her that she was healed. That relationship changed forever.

That was me. That is me! That woman is me! When I read that as a young girl it was the faith of the woman that amazed me. As I read it as a woman with Lupus, a blood disorder, it is the love of the Savior that amazes me. He knows who we are and He wants to help us overcome our challenges in life and have a relationship with us. He wants us to know who He is, but also wants us to know that He knows who we are, too. He knows us.

Chapter 2

HERE AM I, SEND ME!

Now the Lord had shown unto me, Abraham, the intelligences that were organized before the world was; and among all these there were many of the noble and great ones;

And God saw these souls that they were good, and he stood in the midst of them, and he said: these I will make my rulers; for he stood among those that were spirits, and he saw that they were good; and he said unto me: Abraham, thou are one of them; thou wast chosen before thou was born.

And there stood one among them that was like unto God, and he said unto those who were with him: We will go down, for there is space there, and we will take of these materials, and we will make an earth whereon these may dwell;

And we will prove them herewith, to see if they will do all things whatsoever the Lord their God shall command them;

And they who keep their first estate shall be added upon; and they who keep not their first estate shall not have glory in the same kingdom with those who keep their first estate; and they who keep their second estate shall have glory added upon their heads forever and ever.

And the Lord said: Whom shall I send? And one answered like unto the Son of Man: Here am I, send me. And another answered and said: Here am I, send me. And the Lord said: I will send the first.

And the second was angry, and kept not his first estate; and, at that day, many followed after him.

Abraham 3:22-28 (Pearl of Great Price)

In the Church of Jesus Christ of Latter Day Saints, one may be asked to serve in a certain calling, and that individual is given the chance to accept the calling or decline it. After accepting the calling, the bishop announces this in a Sacrament meeting among the congregation when we all get to sustain and show our love and support for the individual for accepting the call. We all have a purpose in this life, and are called to do something great. Now, discovering what that calling is and accepting it may take a lifetime for some of us; yet we all have the potential to do great things in this life in many different ways.

I don't remember the pre-mortal life—no one does, or that would defeat the purpose of God's plan and the purpose of faith. However, I would like to think that as we each received our mission in life, it was similar to how we are called to serve in the church. I know that I was given an earthly calling from my Father in Heaven to do something great. I don't know the details; I don't know if I even listened to the Lord when and if He gave me details in the pre-mortal life. I can say that knowing the person that I am today, and my excitement for the Gospel, I was happy just to hear that I will have the opportunity to do this; to come to Earth and experience life with its trials and triumphs, gain a body, an eternal family, knowledge, and to grow closer to becoming like Father in Heaven. I think I just said yes before even hearing the details of it all. I also think it was just as our Savior volunteered when He said, "Here am I, send me." (Abraham 3:27). We've all had the opportunity to say the same thing for something special that needs to happen or be experienced in the plan for each of our lives. I don't know the details, but I do know that in the beginning I had to have said, "Here am I, send me," and was happy about it.

I am happy to be living and experiencing what I am at this time of my life, despite the hardships. As a child, I didn't know about the plan of salvation or understand it. As I have accepted the Gospel of Jesus Christ in its fullness, I understand who I am and why I'm here. I know where I'm going and I am happy. This is what I want to share with people! It will bring them peace and happiness in this life and eternal joy in the next.

I was introduced to the sister missionaries from the Church of Jesus Christ of Latter Day Saints when I was 15 years old. I was at a point in my life when I was searching for more; searching for instructions and guidance to help me through the challenges I was facing at that time. I always read the Bible, and everyone who knew me, knew how much I came to love the Lord and everything about Him. So when the sister missionaries first taught me the discussion about our Heavenly Father and His plan of salvation (or another name is plan of happiness), it all rang true and familiar to my heart. I knew that it was the truth. After much prayer and pondering, despite the wishes of my family, I decided to get baptized. I am ever so grateful I followed the promptings of the Holy Ghost instead of falling under the pressure of family members who were trying to discourage me from getting baptized with reasons that didn't have a sound foundation.

When one knows that something is right and true, when the power of the Holy Ghost reveals truth to one's heart, it's kind of hard to deny that feeling. It takes a great amount of effort to shut that feeling of truth down. It's definitely possible, and one can ignore it, but once you feel it, it's a sure thing that doesn't leave doubt in your mind or heart. It just leaves you with a choice of accepting or refusing it. I chose to accept it, for it's what I'd been looking for and waiting on for a very long time.

In 2002, I applied to go on a mission for the church. I received my call in letter form to go to serve in the Fiji Suva Mission, speaking French. I was to report to the Missionary Training Center (MTC) in January 2003. The following is my journal entry a few weeks before leaving my family.

December 5, 2002 (Edited)

I am the middle child of three children. I have one sister and one brother. My momma can be my best friend at times. Then at other times … she makes me really mad, and I'm sure I make her mad, too. I haven't heard from or about my dad in seven years. I always think of him and put his name on the prayer roll in the temple.

My sister and I don't have the best of relationships but her children, my nephews and my niece, is what makes me love to be around her. I love my nephews and niece.

I am closer to my brother than anybody else in this family. He's one year younger than I am and I love him so much. He's about to welcome a new baby into his family. She will be born in a few weeks. There are people in this family that I care about so much, it's painful to see them go on without having the Gospel in their lives.

I am the only active member of the church in our family. My mom was baptized two years after me but she's inactive.

My brother was baptized two years after her and he's inactive, too, but he does read the Bible and the Book of Mormon a lot with his girlfriend. He's naming his daughter Sariah, after the mother of the prophet Nephi that is spoken of in the Book of Mormon.

Two months ago I got my mission call to serve in Fiji. At first I was confused, but I now really do feel like this is where I'm supposed to go. The Lord can send me anywhere and I will serve Him to the best of my ability. I leave for the MTC in five weeks, Jan 15, 2003.

Being baptized into this church is one of the best things that has happened to me in this life. Like I tell many, I would have never joined this church if I didn't know with a surety that it's the Lord's church restored upon the earth. The Book of Mormon has opened my mind; showed me the impossible made possible. It has enriched me with knowledge and wisdom. I know that the Book of Mormon is true. I know that Joseph Smith was a true prophet. He saw the Lord and there was no way he could deny that. As it is with me; there is no way I could deny the truth. This is my testimony!

Chapter 3

THE START OF IT ALL

There have been occasions in my life, especially if I was sitting too long, when I would feel this pain in my side. It was some kind of an annoying cramp that wouldn't go away unless I rested. It would only last for a day or two, if that. So when I started feeling this familiar pain on my mission, I tried to ignore it, thinking it wasn't a big deal.

We do a lot of walking on our mission and I was sure this is why I had started to feel the pain in my side; but the pain wasn't going away, it was getting worse.

It was a beautiful, hot and humid July day in New Caledonia; nothing different from any other hot day on the island. I had been on my mission for six months already. Soeur (Sister) Sally, my companion, and I, had a couple of appointments that were in the squats. The squats were another name that we called the jungle. It was full of trees, mud, mosquitoes, and the humble. People who lived in the squats may have seemed like they didn't have much, but they were the most pleasant and kindest people on the island. They were also the most open to listening to us missionaries. I loved going to the squats for them, but I hated traveling there because of the bugs and mud, and sometimes it took forever to get to your destination with all the walking. If you didn't know your way around the squats then you would definitely get lost, because there were no road signs or directions, just a jungle.

I didn't realize that something was seriously wrong with my body until we continued to walk through the squats looking for our investigator's home. We'd been walking for five or ten minutes when the pain I felt in my side was overshadowed by the pain I was feeling in my chest whenever I would breathe. My backpack was too much to carry and I just felt weak and tired. I didn't bother to mention any of this to my companion just yet.

We finally got to our investigator's home and were sitting on the sofa. I could barely get air into my lungs because it hurt to inhale, especially when I was sitting down. I said a quiet prayer, asking Heavenly Father to help me. Somehow I made it through that discussion; in fact, I don't think I even said much, but allowed Soeur Sally to do all the talking and teaching.

We went to another investigator's home in the squats right after that. We didn't stay long, but we did have a prayer with him and his family. I remember still struggling with pain as I took breaths, but it wasn't as bad when I knelt to participate in the prayer instead of sitting on the floor. As we were leaving the squats heading to the car, I told my companion that I wanted to go home to take a Tylenol because I wasn't feeling well, I explained to her the pain I was feeling and that I might have to go to the doctor. I don't remember our conversation in detail, but my desire to serve was stronger than my desire to stop and rest and get better. However, I knew that I couldn't go to another appointment without taking a Tylenol.

Once I got home I took the Tylenol in hopes that it would take the edge off the pain I was feeling. Then I got on my knees beside my bed to say a prayer. I needed to ask God for His help with this one because this was something I had never felt before. I'm not just speaking of the pain, but a change that was coming that left me a little unsure of what was happening to me.

As I knelt down and collected my thoughts, I felt a gentle and calm feeling come over me. Then the thought came, *"This is it, this is the start of it all, but don't worry, Father will be with you."* I said my prayer, having the Spirit help me to know what to say. I don't remember every word of my prayer, but I do remember how confident I felt about a change that was about to happen. I remember asking the Lord for strength to get through it and helping me to trust in His will for my life. I knew that whatever was about to happen was part of the plan for my life and I was ready. I ended my prayer with the words of our Savior when He was in the Garden of Gethsemane suffering for us, "Not my will, but thy will be done." (Luke 22:42)

When I got off my knees, I went to my companion and she asked if we should walk to our next appointment instead of taking the car. This was because we were only allowed to put so many miles on the car a day and we were either reaching our limit or already there. I really didn't want to walk. I knew that if we walked, I wasn't going to make it back home, but I didn't tell her that. I just wanted to go with the flow, so I agreed to walk. It was a distance, but one straight shot, all downhill, and no jungle. The walk there wasn't as bad.

Once we got to our appointment, the Tylenol had started to work. I still felt pain in my side but breathing was okay; until I accepted the offer of a cold glass of Coca Cola. Our friend (investigator) offered us cheese balls and soda. I hadn't had soda for months and I usually don't drink it, but, man, it was a taste that I didn't mind being reminded of—though I will never forget what it did to me that night.

Once I took a sip, I jumped up off the couch in pain, gasping for air. I couldn't breathe because the pain in my chest was so severe. The tears came and I couldn't speak. My companion and our friend immediately came to me, trying to figure out what was wrong. All I could manage to get out in bits and pieces was, "I … can't … breathe." I held on tightly to my companion, pleading for help with my body language because I felt like somebody was suffocating me. It was horrible, the worst pain I had ever felt.

In the middle of all that, I somehow was able to calm down to catch more deep breaths. Actually they weren't deep breaths, just quick and small breaths that kept me going. I couldn't sit. I just stayed standing while holding onto my companion as she called several people (on the phone) trying to find us a ride to the hospital. Soeur Sally finally got a hold of President Mou-Tham, who was the acting mission president in New Caledonia while President Woolley, the mission president for our whole mission, was in Nandi, Fiji. President Mou-Tham showed up and drove us to the hospital. I was in so much pain that it took me a while to be able to get into the car. I was okay standing. The pain was still there whenever I would inhale, but I could get some air here and there. Whenever I bent over or had to sit or lay down, I couldn't breathe or didn't want to breathe at all because of the pain. So it was more of them having to force me into the car because my body wouldn't allow me to do it voluntarily with the pain. It was so painful … so very painful.

We got to the hospital and I was able to tolerate sitting in a wheelchair, but as soon as they put me in a bed and tried to make me lay down, I couldn't handle it. I was yelling in pain. I made the doctors and nurses around me very nervous. It was kind of funny, now that I think about it; they were French-speaking people trying to help me and I was making them uncomfortable. I wasn't being dramatic on purpose, but really in pain. I think they may have thought that I was being over-dramatic. The doctor who spoke English told me that I couldn't yell because I was scaring the other patients. I told him in anger that I was in pain and I couldn't lie down because it hurt. The doctor seemed annoyed with me and I was definitely annoyed with them because I felt like they didn't understand what I was feeling—or saying, for that matter. I definitely didn't feel like the doctor had any empathy at all, but it was probably because he didn't know what was going on with me. I wasn't comfortable either, being in a hospital with a bunch of people who didn't speak my language and couldn't understand what I needed or was saying to them. It was an experience. But they finally calmed me down by allowing me to sit up in the bed and giving me something for the pain.

*Some names changed due to confidentiality.

Chapter 4

A CALLING WITHIN A CALLING

(Journal entries from the last three months of my mission.
Some names have been changed due to confidentiality.)
July 25 to October 2003

In the beginning, I had a desire to serve a mission. The definition of a mission to me is when a person goes and teaches others about Jesus Christ and His love for us. I had a desire to teach people what I'd learned. I wanted to help them know the truth and bear my testimony about it. That was my goal since I'd joined the church; to go on a mission.

As the time became closer, I realized that it was one of the steps I had to take for the plan of my life. I knew that I couldn't progress in life without first going on a mission. I received my call, I departed, I am here, I am doing, but now something is happening and I'm not sure if I know what it is. I serve, yes, but it's a different kind of service.

The Lord had told me to just be obedient. That's what I am doing. I am just being obedient because I don't know any other thing to do. Yes, I would love to go out and teach all the time, but that's not what He is asking from me. That's okay; my #1 priority and desire is to do what He asks me to do. I will go and do whatever He desires of me because I love Him, and I know that His way is the best way. I just wish sometimes I could see what He is doing, what He is trying to accomplish so that I can understand better. But I know that's when I need to have faith and patience. I know God lives and He is in control.

I will be obedient and do what He asks of me. I say this in the name of Jesus Christ, Amen! (Journal from August 2003)

July 25, 2003 (Edited)

Wow! I have a lot to write, so much to say, but I don't think I can say it all. Last Wednesday night I went to the hospital because I couldn't breathe or move. We stayed at the hospital for three and a half hours and they sent me home. I slept that night for two hours and I couldn't move or breathe anymore because of the pain (that returned). It was horrible. I never in my life want to suffer like that again. Soeur Sally called the Elders to come and give me a blessing. It was 3:00 a.m. on Thursday and four of the Elders came and gave me a blessing. The pain became bearable and I was able to breathe normally. It was indeed a blessing/miracle to me.

By 8:00 a.m. they took me back to the hospital because the pain had returned and I couldn't go on. I stayed in the hospital for a week. Today I go home. I did a lot of tests, and the doctors found that I had an infection and fluid around my lungs that was causing most of my pain. They stuck a needle in my back and drained the fluid out; it was a lot. I still have a lung infection, but they gave me medication to help heal it.

My companions have been a great support to me; so have the Elders. The Lord knew that this was going to happen and He made a way for me to get it taken care of. This experience has taught me that He has His hands in every detail and He is constantly watching over us.

I can breathe a lot better now. It's my first night home so hopefully all goes well and I sleep well. We have two of the other sisters here with us who have been helping Soeur Sally continue with the work and who have been staying with me at the hospital. They'll be getting transferred to their new sector (area) tomorrow.

Tomorrow is the missionary's zone conference and everyone will get to see one another. Tomorrow evening is also the baptism of Anna. Well, I'm feeling lightheaded and a little tired so I'm going to close now with I am grateful that I am home. I am grateful to be doing the Lord's will. I love my Savior with all my heart and I want to say more, but later. I say these things in the name of Jesus Christ, Amen.

July 26, 2003 (Edited)

Today is Saturday. I went to the zone conference and it was good to see all the Elders again. I learned that last Friday all the missionaries fasted for me to get better.

Before I got sick, I was starting to feel very close to Soeur Sally. She is like my sister, my true sister, and that's because we bonded a lot. After not being with her for 10 days and she being with another companion, I don't feel as close to her anymore. I felt like I would have to start all over with her again. But today when we talked, it helped me to know that nothing changed with our relationship; I was happy.

I was told by the doctor that I couldn't move around as much and had to be on bed rest for one week. I feel okay; I feel like I can go teach people. Maybe not like I used to do, but I can still teach.

We have two sisters who are staying with us to help out, Sister Shay and Sister Thompson. Yes, I get jealous because it's my job to do this or that, and I hate it when someone comes and takes over. I did humble myself because one, I don't have the strength for competition, and two, I don't like to compete. The Lord made us all different and gave us all different talents so I have no reason to compare my works with Soeur Shay, Sally, Thompson, or any other sister or person. We are all here to help the Lord build up His kingdom on the Earth.

So right now I am here at home in bed, being babysat by Soeur Shay while Soeur Thompson and Soeur Sally are at a family home evening with investigators. I miss the nurses who were in the hospital with me. They were very kind people. We are going back on Thursday because I have to get another x-ray. I haven't told my family or friends about it yet. What they don't know won't hurt them, right?!

Today was the baptism of Anna. She is so sweet and the Spirit was so strong there. I had to bear my testimony. I was weak physically and short of breath, but I did it. I learned that when I try to apply a personal experience with my testimony, it makes it so much better. I bore my testimony of how the Lord is always there. I actually love telling my personal experiences in French now because it makes the story so much better, humble and spiritual. I guess it's because I don't know French that well, so I rely on the Lord more.

This past week went by fast and it seemed like two days ago I just went to the hospital. I've learned a lot by having this experience. I have seen a lot of miracles. The baptism of Anna was really special. I was glad I was able to be there and be a special witness of that ordinance. I love my Heavenly Father and I know He loves me. He lives, and I know this without a doubt. I say this in Jesus' name, Amen.

July 28, 2003

Today is P-Day. I went on a split with the other sisters to help clean their new apartment while my companion went with another sister to help paint an investigator's apartment. I think I did a little bit too much because I'm hurting now and I feel very weak. We also went to the chapel to spend time with the other missionaries.

My companion is having a hard time now. She's feeling discouraged and wants a shoulder to cry on. I'm not good at comforting people; I just know how to tell the truth and that's all. I tried to have a listening ear, but I don't think I helped at all. Les autres Sœurs sont a chez elles maintenant. (The other sisters are at their house now.)

I just want to add a little bit of my feelings about my mission. It was hard the first couple of days after I got out of the hospital because I didn't know where I stood. I didn't know what was expected of me. I would wake up in the morning and just pray that I could just close my eyes and be somewhere else, or I would wake up in the middle of the night praying that morning wouldn't come. I just didn't want to go on like this. But each time I prayed, I would feel the Spirit tell me that I could do it, and I will do it, and the Lord will always be there to help me. I would feel that I was never alone. Sure enough, each day I did it the best that I could and the Lord was always there.

I'm learning to put my faith in God at all times and make Him my master and my boss. As long as I put my trust in Him, I will be okay. I try not to compare myself with the other missionaries and I have been doing a good job at that. I simply try to do the best I can each day, hoping that today is better than yesterday … or tomorrow will be better than today.

I love my Savior and I know that He loves me, too. I know He lives and He has a plan for me and you. All that is required on our part is to listen and obey; then He will light the road so that we can see the way. I know that the Gospel is true. I know it without a doubt. This is my testimony, humbly and sincerely in the name of Jesus Christ, Amen.

July 30, 2003 (Edited)

Today is Wednesday, and it was really hard getting up this morning. Actually, it's been mentally hard to do anything I'm supposed to do. I'm just getting a little bit tired of life going the same way each day. Health-wise … I'm okay. I have to get an x-ray Friday and see what the doctor says. I think I will be fine.

In two more days we will be in the month of August. I can hardly believe it. At times, this year feels like it's going by so fast, and then at other times it feels like it's not going fast enough. I've lost a lot of weight since I was in the hospital. I lost about 20-25 pounds, so needless to say, I need to go buy new skirts and dresses next week; that's exciting.

Today we are starting out late because I slept in till 8:30-9:00 a.m. I had to rest. It was really difficult to think about getting out of bed. I haven't heard from my family, but that's nothing new for me. Rudell writes me all the time and I have to write her back soon. Other than that, life is the same for me. I have a desire to teach people, but first we have to find them. Soeur Sally doesn't do a lot of street contact here like I did in PK7. Yesterday I stopped a woman on the street to start teaching her and Soeur Sally wasn't very supportive, but that's okay. She's always supporting me in everything else. She is a good companion and I'm grateful to have her. She loves to serve people and indeed, she is a true servant of the Lord.

Well, I have to read my Scriptures and prepare to go out and do my best with teaching. I just want to add that I am so grateful for the love of my Heavenly Father. Sometimes I'm scared to take another step or I have no idea what to do or say next. Sometimes I feel completely alone and unprepared for an upcoming situation. But I will testify that each time I felt these feelings, He always took me by my hand and led the way. He is always there and He always makes things better. That's how I managed to get up this morning and each morning, because I depend on His love and His guiding counsel. I know He lives and I say this in Jesus' name, Amen.

August 4, 2003 (First Part, Edited)

Friday I went to the doctor to get another x-ray, and they saw that my lungs were better. The doctor then told me that I don't have a lung infection but I have some type of blood disease. I really didn't understand anything he said because it was all in French. He said that I have to get more exams done … He also wants me to see a specialist for my kidneys. I don't think he knows what he's talking about because I don't feel unhealthy. Yes, I still hurt, but nothing like before. I don't know what's wrong with me, but I don't feel like it's anything serious.

He told me that I have three options and it's my choice. First, I can stay here and do the exams and get treatments. Second, I can go to Australia and get it done faster and in English. Third, I can go back home and get it done. I started feeling a lot of things when he said that. I spoke to President Woolley, the mission president, because I wanted to know how I was going to pay for all this and he told me not to worry about it. And of course, I am. He told me that I might have to get sent closer to home.

Honestly, I don't feel like an instrument in the Lord's hands here. Soeur Sally does everything. All the other missionaries have things to do and the health, time, and language. Me? … I don't know why I've been called because I don't get to teach much and I don't feel that the Lord uses me. He knew that I had a desire to teach; He knew that I wanted to serve him. He called me here . . . why? I can't speak the language that well. I don't get much opportunity to teach. I really don't have anything to do and now my health is failing. I don't like where I am, and I don't like what I am doing. I want to teach, and I want to teach by the Spirit. I feel like the Lord gives everybody else what they desire but me . . . why? Why doesn't He give me what I desire? I just desire to teach the Gospel in my language by the Spirit. I want to feel the Spirit and I want to see the change of heart of that investigator.

Many would say I lack faith, and others would say that I am ungrateful. I just simply say that I don't know what He wants from me. Yes, I desire to do His will, but He doesn't tell me anything. Yes, I'm hoping that I will get the opportunity to get transferred closer to home and speak English, for this is what I want to do!

August 4, 2003 (Second Part, Edited)

I just got back from teaching an investigator who is from New Zealand. She speaks English, so we got to teach her in English. It went well. I felt the Spirit there and I know she did, too. I love teaching in English. I love teaching in my language. I love to teach, and I don't get to do much of that, especially in my language. I know I can't see what God can see. I know that if I really want to serve the Lord, then I will do what He wants me to do and not what I want to do.

Right now I'm just having a hard time with that because He knows how much I want to teach people about Him. He knew that I chose to go on a mission because I wanted to teach and testify of Him and His work. Why is it going this way? How come He doesn't tell me what's going on? Doesn't He care about my wants and desires? I have righteous desires. It doesn't matter; I'm going to do what He wants me to do anyway, whether I like it or not, whether I understand or not. Why? Because He's my Father and I love Him, and I will serve Him in whatever way He wants me to. I love Him, and I can never deny His love for me. I know He knows more than I do and He knows what's best for me, but I still have high hopes that if the opportunity arrives for me to get transferred to another mission closer to home (English-speaking), I'm taking it.

August 14, 2003 (Edited)

I have some things to share. Two days ago I was in a really good mood and I had an experience I wanted to share but I never took time to write in my journal. Monday I e-mailed my sister about my health because the doctors wanted to know about my family health history.

The next day my sister called the mission office in Fiji and talked to President Woolley's wife. Sister Woolley told my sister that I would call her. President Woolley called me on Tuesday and told me to call my family; I tried, but no one was at home. So yesterday (Wednesday) I tried again several times and no one was at home. An hour or two later I got a call from the mission office and they told me to call home because my sister called again and left an intense message on the phone wanting to hear from me.

I called again for the last time and I got a hold of my momma. She was so happy to hear from me and I was happy to hear from her. She called Grandma and we were on a 3-way call. My momma told me that Terrance wanted to talk to me, but I couldn't talk to anybody for a long time. I told them how I was doing and that I was going to be okay. My momma wanted me to come back home. I told her that I wasn't unless I had to get surgery or something and I know that I don't need that. I don't have a long time left on my mission, so I told her I was going to finish it here. I didn't get to speak to my sister because she was working. I was glad to hear from my momma and Grandma. No one writes me so it was good to hear them. I will be able to call them again, I'm sure, sometime next month, to tell them the results, and I will be able to talk to them again on Christmas in four months.

As far as my mission is going, well, I'd rather talk about that another day. I have to read my Scriptures right now. It's been nine weeks since I've been with Soeur Sally; yes, we've been having some rough times lately. I just hope it gets better.

August 20, 2003 (Catherine and Pierre, Edited)

I want to tell about this family we met by doing port à port (door to door contact) in the squats a month ago. We met Catherine. She is Melanesian and comes from Lifou, another island. We first taught Catherine with her cousin, Elizabeth. When we finished, we asked if we could come back to teach her more and she said no. My heart sank. I started to feel like I felt with Paul (another investigator). I knew the Gospel was what she was looking for and I knew she needed it. I began to testify to her about the love our Heavenly Father has for her and how He is waiting to give her so many gifts and blessings. I felt the Spirit strong with Catherine and I asked her again if we could come back to teach her more about her Heavenly Father and she said yes. I felt joy that day; but that's not all.

The next time we went back, her husband was there. He looked so familiar, and then he told us that he knew me from the hospital. He works in the hospital as a transporter, and when I was there he took me to my different appointments. I knew then that the Lord had led us to that house. They listened to us teach, they listened to us sing. Catherine loves when we sing. They invited us to come back and teach them more. They invited us to come back and eat with them. Each time I left that family I felt a special, warm feeling in my heart. I know that the Lord is with them and He will help them come unto Him, even Christ. I love that family.

Catherine is about 25 or 26 and Pierre is about the same age. They have a 2-year-old boy named Eddie and about a 7-month-old baby girl. They had another daughter who died when she was a baby. I know this family is searching; they are searching for the love of God and answers to the many questions they have. That family is so special to me. I will keep an update on what's happening each time we go see them.

August 20, 2003 (Jean-Pierre, Edited)

Jean-Pierre is another special *ami* (investigator) of ours. We met Jean-Pierre in the squats, too. Soeur Sally and I didn't have anything to do. We didn't have any set appointments. So I said, "Well, let's do port à port here." She laughed at me, but I meant it. It's hard to do port à port literally in the squats because some of the humble homes have no door. Anyway, we decided to do it.

A man came along and he greeted us with, "Bonjour," and we greeted in return, "Bonjour." Soeur Sally looked at me and she hesitated to go after him but I ran after him, waving for Soeur Sally to follow. I stopped the man and began to talk a little, then Soeur Sally came and we started a little conversation with him. We talked about Joseph Smith, and Jean-Pierre said that he knew about Joseph Smith and that he even had a Book of Mormon that Elders had given to him some years ago. Jean-Pierre invited us to come and teach his family and we ended with a prayer.

The next time we went to see him it was the night that I first went to the hospital. I didn't see him for a long time, but Soeur Sally went back to visit him with Soeur Thompson. After I got out of the hospital we went to see him; they are a family who believes in praying all the time. They love the Lord so much. We even went to his prayer meeting and taught his pastor, who also studied with the Elders at the beginning of this year. We taught his pastor the third discussion and about Joseph Smith and his pastor said that he will pray about it.

We taught Jean-Pierre about baptism; he'd never been baptized. He said that baptism is something very important and he wants to make sure that he understands the things he must do before he gets baptized. He is so sincere. He knows that there is something missing and it's the authority from God to baptize. He seems to recognize the Spirit easily.

Last Saturday we went to teach him again about the Book of Mormon. He wanted to know the But (purpose, pronounced BUTE) for this life and if he would be with his family forever. We taught him the plan of salvation, and he said that he knows that it is true. I gave him a Scripture out of the Book of Mormon, Ether 4:12, and he cried. He cried when he read that Scripture. He told us that he knows the Book of Mormon is true. We invited him to come to church on Sunday and he said that he will pray about all the things we'd just taught him. He wants to make sure it's the right thing to do. He felt the Spirit. I know that one day soon, Jean-Pierre will accept the Gospel and come unto Christ by being baptized by one who has the authority. I have faith and hope in him. We have another appointment next Saturday; I can hardly wait!

Although I may feel the Spirit with many of these investigators and have high hopes that they'll come unto Christ, I've also had the experiences of those who have felt the Spirit testify to them the truth and still would say "no more, no, I don't want it anymore." Those times are really hard for me and I don't understand, but I can't give up. I must not give up, and I must not fear man's rejections. I must remember who I am working for and whose field I am working in. I must do my part and I must do it to the best of my ability. I love those who live in the squats. They are meek and humble, they are lowly in heart, and they are poor in temporal things but rich in spiritual things. I know that my mission can be hard and complicated at times, but it's moments like these, teaching moments with those who are searching diligently, that make the hard times and complicated times worth it!!!

August 28, 2003 (Catherine and Pierre, Update)

Yesterday we had an appointment with Catherine and Pierre. We taught them the plan of salvation and we ate dinner with them. I felt the Spirit there so strongly when we were teaching and they were really interested. As we ate dinner with them a thought came into my head. *Why are they being so nice to us? What if at the end of dinner they tell us that they are not interested, what will I do? How will I react?* Then I felt that I would just bear my testimony and tell them that it's their choice. Well, guess what? After we all finished dinner, Pierre said that he wanted to continue to read the Book of Mormon, but he didn't want us to come back for a while. He didn't want us coming back every day, but once every two weeks. I knew that was going to happen. We agreed and we were grateful he didn't want to stop discussing completely. They are very nice to us and I just feel the Spirit whenever I am around them.

I just want to bear my testimony that I know my Savior lives. I know that He sees each of us and He loves us. Yes, the Gospel would be so much easier to teach in my own language; He knows that and I know that. But in English or French it doesn't matter, my testimony is the same. I love the Lord and I will stand strong and I will do my very best. I know that when I can't go on, He will be there to help me. I have eternal goals. My treasures are set in heaven, where no man can steal them. It is the love of Jesus Christ that keeps me going. It's His mercy and His unconditional love. This is my testimony in the name of Jesus Christ, Amen.

September 26, 2003 (Edited)

A lot has happened spiritually, emotionally, and physically with me. First I want to say that Soeur Noble is a great companion. She makes Soeur Sally and me laugh all the time. She's 58 years old and has been a convert to the church for 37 years. She lost her husband when she was 33 years old. She has a strong testimony of the Gospel and a great sense of humor. I am always laughing with her.

It's been a little hard being in a three-person companionship. Soeur Noble has bad knees so she can't always walk up and down the stairs when we have amies (friends/investigators) who live on the fifth floor. She has a good attitude about it. We can't ... well, usually we've been coming home early at night, like 6:00 p.m., because Soeur Noble doesn't feel so well after walking and climbing stairs all day. I give her a big pat on the back for doing as much as she does. I know she suffers, but she fights it. She is a great woman. Her French is not all that good. She only stayed in the MTC (Mission Training Center) for 10 days so she really doesn't know how to speak the language. She understands better each day. I'm surprised with myself because I translate for her at the discussions and I didn't know I could do that. The Lord has blessed me so much. He has given me the gift of tongues and interpretation of tongues and I am so grateful. No, my French isn't anywhere near perfect, but I can understand well and I can speak good enough to gain a relationship with the investigator and teach the Gospel.

I am also thankful for my good old companion, Soeur Sally. She is truly my sister. I've learned a lot with her and from her. I couldn't have asked the Lord for a better companion. Time has been so good to us and we have been together since June 16, so almost four months. She is a wonderful girl, a great missionary, and indeed, a friend to me.

Physically, I was doing well, but I don't know now. Since I got out of the hospital, each week there has been one thing on my body that has been aching. Each week it's something different, and I think I may have something wrong with my nerves. I may have a pinched nerve. Anyway, yesterday my back started hurting on the upper right side and I just ignored it because I thought it would go away, like all the other times. Last night it started to get unbearable so I took two Tylenols and I still felt the pain, but it was bearable. At 3:00 a.m. I got up to use the bathroom and I thought I was going to die because of the pain. The same thing happened this morning at six thirty. I got down on my knees and asked the Lord for help. I don't know what's wrong with me, I just know that I want to serve my Father and do His will. I love the Gospel and I love my Lord and I say this in the name of Jesus Christ, Amen.

October 4, 2003 (Edited)

I just want to say that I love my family and I like my life. I only have a short time here with my two companions and I should make the best of it.

I spoke to Elder Zane yesterday and it helped me to feel better letting someone know that this companionship is having trouble. He knows now that I can't teach or go on this way. He encouraged me and told me that he'd already written a transfer and faxed it to President Woolley. President Woolley okayed it but it won't take place until after I go to the hospital. Oh, the kidney doctor wants me to come in for an appointment next Thursday and he wants me to do a kidney biopsy; therefore, I will have to be in the hospital for two days.

Elder Zane told me that when I get out, I would be in another three-person companionship. I pleaded with him to change that. I did not or do not want to have two companions. It's too difficult for me. He told me not to worry, but that he will speak to President Woolley again.

I told President Woolley that this is not how I expected a mission to be. He told me that there isn't a certain mission. Everyone has a different mission.

I just want to conclude by saying that I'm grateful to be in the Lord's service. It's hard at times, but it's worth it. Yesterday we did a split. Soeur Noble went to stay with Soeur Shay because she (Shay) is sick, and Soeur Thompson came with us. I had a wonderful experience. We went to visit an old investigator who is from the Philippines and speaks English. I got to teach in my own language and I got to feel the Spirit literally tell me what to say. It was bold and strong, but it was true and loving. It was true, and every person in that room was shocked and amazed. They were all staring at me as if to say, "WOW! Where did that come from?" At first I started to feel like I was a little too bold, but that feeling quickly passed and I did not deny what I had said. I felt the Spirit, and I'm grateful the Lord used me as an instrument in His hands.

He puts a lot of trust in us as missionaries and we are responsible to do His will. We are His servants, and I want to do the very best I can. I'm not perfect, but my intentions are good. I love the Lord and I am grateful for the Gospel in my life.

October 10, 2003 (First Part, Edited)

Here I go again. Yesterday I went to the doctor and he told me that I have a disease that will never go away, called Lupus. It's a blood disease that can become threatening to my life if I don't start treating it. He also said that my kidneys aren't looking too good and that he needs to do a biopsy to see what is wrong with them. I'll be in the hospital for a day or two; but that's not all the news.

Yesterday I also spoke to the AP (assistant to the president), Elder Zane, and he told us the transfers. Soeur Howard and Soeur Milly will be coming to stay with me in my sector and Soeur Sally and Soeur Noble will be going to PK7. They'll still work in the office. Soeur Howard will be the senior companion . . . I won't share my feelings about that right now. I just want to say that I feel so overwhelmed. I don't want to do this anymore!

October 10, 2003 (Second Part, Edited)

I'm here at the hospital waiting to get a room. I'm not nervous at all. I'm not afraid. I just want it to take forever. I really wish I could stay in the hospital forever. I don't want to return home (mission home). I guess you can say that I'm losing my desire to continue to do this work. It's only been nine months since I've been on my mission. I do have the desire to teach. I think I will always have that desire, but not here, not in this situation. I wouldn't mind serving or finishing my mission in the United States.

We had a problem this morning with our companionship again. Soeur Noble has no desire to be with Soeur Sally, and I have no desire to be with Soeur Howard again. I never thought a mission was like this. I just don't want to do it anymore. I truly don't. I don't want to leave this hospital because I don't want to go back in the field this way.

Soeur Noble and Soeur Sally will be staying with me in the hospital during the day but tonight I can't have anyone with me. I'm glad it will be that way because I just want a break from it all. Well, I can't really share my feelings the way I want to. All I can say is that whatever happens … happens. I'm tired of fighting and struggling and I don't want to do it anymore. I don't! And I won't!

October 11, 2003 (Edited)

It's done and almost over with. The doctor took a piece of my kidney yesterday and now I'm sore and feel very weird. I have another appointment with him in 15 days and hopefully he can tell me what is wrong with my kidneys. Right now I'm still in the hospital, with Soeur Noble by my side. She refuses to go anywhere with Soeur Sally.

I made my decision as far as my mission goes. I decided that I want to go back to the United States. I want to continue my mission there or I just want to stop completely. I spoke to Soeur Noble about my decision and she surprised me when she agreed with me. In fact, she said that she knew I would. I was comforted. I know it's time for me to go home. I don't know really what I'll do or how I'll do it. I just know that I received my answer. As soon as I get out of the hospital I will go and call President Woolley and request to go home.

I don't care anymore about being companions with Soeur Howard again. I'm glad we'll have Soeur Milly there to help us. I talked to Elder Zane, the AP, again last night, and I asked him why it is that Sister Howard is coming to my sector being senior. He said that President Woolley prayed about it and this is what the Lord wants. He also told me it's obvious that I will be the leader because I've been in this sector for four months, but it's nothing I should be worrying about because I might leave soon. I was shocked to hear him say that. That also confirmed my decision to go home.

This mission has taught me so much, and now that I have this Lupus disease for the rest of my life, I think my own personal goals will change. I never had a health problem until I came on my mission. It's okay; it's all in the Lord's plan. A calling within a calling! I hope I can continue to do the best I can and serve. I say this in the name of Jesus Christ, Amen!

October 14, 2003 (First Part, Edited)

The changes have been made. I'm here in my same area with Soeur Howard and Soeur Milly. Yesterday was hard; I didn't know what to do or how to carry on. I just said a prayer and then I went and communicated with Soeur Howard. It went okay. Soeur Milly is good to speak to. I'm grateful she is here too. Yesterday was still hard for me because I felt lost, confused, overwhelmed, uncomfortable, and tired. I can remember wanting to cry several times yesterday. It's very humbling.

I spoke to President Woolley yesterday and he said that he wanted a branch missionary to stay with me. So today there will be four of us here just until Friday. I feel so stressed and overwhelmed, I don't want to think about any of this anymore. I've been praying about telling President Woolley that I want to serve in the States and I've been feeling different things. I can't even focus right; my mind is not on the work like it used to be. All I can say is I'll do my very best and try to make the right choice. I'm tire and overwhelmed and I'm ready to go back home.

I love the Gospel and I love teaching, but I don't have the desire anymore to do it. I tried my best and I will continue to do that. I hope Heavenly Father will allow me to feel His love and comfort always. I really don't feel good anymore physically and a little downhill spiritually. I can only do so much. I hope today and this week will be a good week for me. Also for the sisters! I'm trying to stay strong!

October 14, 2003 (Second Part, Edited)

This morning I left this apartment having a lot of hope. I didn't know what we were going to do. I didn't know exactly how to do things, but I just hoped that the Lord would lead us. I was scared and nervous, but I knew I had to go. Well, we went, and as we went, I felt the Spirit and I started to feel like I wanted to go out every day with these sisters to teach. I showed them around the squats so that tomorrow they could go there while I stayed home with the branch missionary.

Afterwards, we did two contacts on the road and it was great. I was happy. I felt like I couldn't do it before. When I left the house this morning, I didn't feel like a missionary. But now I have that desire to go on and to teach. I personally decided that when the sisters go out tomorrow, Emily and I could go out for a couple of hours to do port à port. I can't stay in this house knowing that I'm still a missionary. The doctor said I have to rest, but I can rest for a couple of hours and then go out for a couple of hours also.

I love teaching. I love doing the Lord's work and if I keep my eyes single to His glory, I know I can do it. I know He will allow me to use my gifts and talents by teaching. I love the Lord. Sometimes it's hard to know His will, but I know that I can't be afraid to act, just do my best. I'm not perfect, but I can take my situation and do the best I can; the best I know! I love the Gospel. I love the opportunity that God has given me at this time. I will be faithful and do the very best I can while time is given to me. I say this in the name of Jesus Christ, Amen!

October 15, 2003 (Edited)

This morning I'm really hurting so I'm going to stay in until 2:30 p.m. Last night was worse, but it's getting better. It's my kidneys that are hurting. It's true that I'm stubborn. I'm stressing, and I bring all of this on my own self. If I have faith and just put it all in the Lord's hands I would be so much better!

Yesterday I went to our district meeting and half of the district was changed. We have two new Elders in our district and Sister Howard and Milly. We lost Elder Arrow; he finished his mission. Elder Zane is no longer in our district. He is still our AP but he changed sectors.

Soeur Milly is a sweet girl. I can grow so close to her. She's so different from me but her humility and her willingness to go and do without having any input is amazing. It was her turn to conduct the companionship study this morning and she didn't have a clue what to do, but she did it. She told me that usually she just goes and does whatever Soeur Howard tells her. I told her please help me by talking to me and letting me know what she thinks about things when we have to make decisions. She told me that she is grateful to be here to see things done differently and not just one way. Soeur Howard is her first companion and was her only companion until now.

Soeur Howard just wants to help. I always misjudge her and will probably do it again whenever she makes me mad, but I also try to look at myself to see if it's just me who is getting easily irritated with her or is it really her. I appreciate Soeur Howard a lot, and I expressed my love and thanks to her last night and this morning. She is really a wonderful person. She is learning, just like everyone else. Soeur Milly is a little quiet at times, but she slowly opens up. She has been out in the field for only two months so she has no clue what is really expected of her. She speaks French really well.

As for me personally, I'm still trying to do the very best I can, and I see the Lord is helping me. I feel His love and I feel His comfort. I spoke to Soeur Sally yesterday and she and I just hugged. I do miss her. She will always be like a sister to me. I learned a lot with her and we always do learn from our companions; especially the ones we have lots of problems with. I spoke to Soeur Noble too, and she said that she and Soeur Sally are still having problems. I encouraged her to have a positive attitude. All three of us were so much alike; independent, stubborn, and wanting to do it our own way. I pray for them all the time and hope they'll learn to love and respect each other.

As far as going home, all I can say is I feel like eventually I will go. I don't know when, but I will go. Sometimes I feel as if I don't want to go. When I do missionary work and feel the Spirit with these people, I want to continue to do this. I love my Lord. I don't know my future, I just know that He knows all things and He love us and just wants us to be happy. He has been my strength and my friend. I love Him with all my heart and I say these things in the name of Jesus Christ, Amen!

October 17, 2003 (Edited)

I'm here at the physical therapist with Sister Milly because she has to get a massage. Her back has been hurting for two months, so yesterday we went to the doctor and he gave her some medicine and instruction to see the physical therapist today.

Soeur Milly has been having a hard time with Soeur Howard as well and she told me that … well, she is just happy to have something different. She was getting depressed because of the way her mission was going. For the past two days, Soeur Milly wanted to go everywhere with me and not with Soeur Howard. I think she is tired of Soeur Howard and just wants a change. She loves Soeur Howard, but she's different. As for me, I am grateful to have Soeur Milly as my companion. I'm grateful for Soeur Howard as well. She is diligent, and she has a certain way of doing things that's not good or bad. Everyone does things differently. I just want everyone to be happy. I don't want to follow or do everything one person's way, but I think we can all work together and get things accomplished much faster and easier.

I may be wrong, but I think Soeur Howard likes to be in charge all the time so she can do things her way, thinking it's the best way. All I'm going to say is that I feel the pain from both Soeur Milly and Soeur Howard. I can understand that Soeur Milly has no desire to be with Soeur Howard anymore or to work with her anymore. Soeur Howard speaks to people like they are her child. She's not a friend, but a mother. I don't think we need that. Then again, I can understand that Soeur Howard doesn't want to feel all alone in doing this work. She wants a companion and she wants to work. I don't have the energy to work or to do anything. I don't have the desire to work like I used to and I'm not sure why.

I was with Soeur Noble and Soeur Sally au jour d'hui (today) and I just … I don't know … I don't feel like I'm in a good situation right now. I have to call the doctor in a few minutes to make an appointment for him to let me know about my kidneys. I'm still having pain. I wish we hadn't made the transfers until after I was better. I know that I'm sick and that I have physical problems, but I don't need or want anyone feeling sorry for me. I don't want to have to answer to anyone, and Soeur Howard sometimes makes people feel like you have to answer to her. Well, not me! Maybe Soeur Milly, but I only tell what I want and when I want. I'm being negative again and that's not good. I'm just going to read my Scriptures and not say a word to anyone. This is my journal entry for today.

October 20, 2003 (First Part, Edited)

I'm in PK7 with Soeur Sally and Soeur Noble right now. I will be here for the week as far as I know. President Woolley called me and he is aware of me deciding to go home. He said that he will call me back this week. It's final, I am going home.

October 20, 2003 (Second Part, Edited)

I have a lot of things to say and I have learned so much. I've noticed feelings that I've had, but was trying to avoid them because of fear that they may be true. I want to start out with the quote in my patriarchal blessing that says: "In time, you will be given the opportunity to serve a mission for the Church of Jesus Christ of Latter Day Saints." I love these two words, *in time.* They can mean so many different little things. Well, I've been told that I have a life-threatening disease called Lupus, which is a blood disease that affects the different organs in my body. I can't be cured from this disease, but I can try to control the pain that it causes me by taking certain medications (steroids, in particular).

When I learned that I would be Sister Howard's companion again I wasn't happy at all. I also was going back into the hospital at that time for a kidney biopsy. It was a very dark, discouraging, depressing, overwhelming, frustrating time for me. When I lay there in the hospital while the doctor did the biopsy on me, I remember just saying to the Lord, "I don't want to do it anymore, Heavenly Father. Please help me." I was afraid of making the wrong choice, yet I knew I couldn't, I just couldn't walk forward anymore knowing that it wasn't what I wanted and it wouldn't be done right. I'm speaking about my situation with becoming companions with Soeur Howard again and having to deal with my health problems. It was too much for me. The only thing that brought peace to me as I lay there in that bed was thinking that it was all going to be okay if I just went home.

After I prayed to Heavenly Father I felt peace; yet I felt a little unsure about whether I'd made the right choice because … well, I knew that it was a good choice but the timing was going to be different. I knew it was okay if I decided to go home, but I also knew that I had to wait until the Lord said to go. Timing is of great importance, I felt.

So, I spoke to Sister Noble that night about my decision and it surprised me how she felt the same way. She told me, "Keela, make sure you are doing it for the right reasons." I told her that I was. I was a little bit impatient with calling President Woolley. I was so excited to have received a confirmation to my answer that I wanted things to take place right away. I knew I wouldn't get a hold of President Woolley, but I had hopes. I also kept feeling that I needed to be patient and wait until the Lord said when to go.

I called President Woolley and he wasn't there. So, that Monday after I was out of the hospital, changes in companionship took place and it was so hard for me. President Woolley called me at home and I didn't tell him about my decision about going home because I followed my feelings that told me to wait. I took one day at a time, holding on firmly to my faith in the Lord's timing and waiting for him to tell me to go.

Every day was so hard for me but I continued and I tried my best. Then on Saturday the 18th of October, I went back to the doctor because I was still feeling pain physically, and of course he gave me more drugs to take. I asked him why I was always tired and discouraged, etc. He said, "Keela, you have an illness. This is not the flu or a cold that can be overcome in a few days or week, but you have a disease." I then realized how sick I was.

The past few days I've been trying to fight with myself to go out every day and teach and do all that a missionary is required to do but my body, my mind, and my emotions were keeping me from doing that. I realized that it's not something I'm choosing to do. I'm not choosing to not do the work, but I really am unable to do it. I tried each day to do my best, but it was literally hard.

Friday night, when I was saying my prayers, I pleaded with the Lord to please help me let go. I'm tired. I couldn't go on this way. It's like when I know that a job has been given to me and I know what's expected of me, but I'm literally unable to do the job. Not because I don't want to, but something that I don't have control over stops me from doing what I always wanted to do. I don't want to do a half-job. If I get up at 6:30 a.m., I want to continue to follow the schedule of the missionaries. I don't want any special privileges. If we have an appointment at 5:00 p.m. and another at 7:00 p.m., well, I want to go out at 5:00 p.m. and stay out until the end of the last appointment. I don't want to just go to the 5:00 p.m. appointment and back home at 6:00 p.m. and go out again at 7:00 p.m. I want to teach with all my heart, my mind, and my strength ... and time.

So, after I finished with the doctor on Saturday morning, I waited out in the lobby with Soeur Noble for Soeur Sally and the other sisters to come and get us. Oh, I wanted to add one more thing about Friday night. After I said my prayers, five minutes later, Soeur Noble and Soeur Sally came to the door dressed up like the Good Samaritan, with chocolate bars in their hands. Soeur Milly, Soeur Shay, and I all got up and turned on the light. We were all shocked to see them. Soeur Howard was in another sector with Sister Thompson while Soeur Shay came to sleep with Soeur Milly and me in our sector. So it was a really good night. But I was still personally having my problems as the sisters talked and joked. I just sat there feeling very tired and overwhelmed. I was still having my personal struggles. Soeur Sally looked over at me and she said, "Soeur Jackson, you look really sick." Everyone laughed because of course I was sick.

I felt like I needed to speak to someone. I needed to hug someone and I needed someone to tell me that it's okay. And not just anyone, but someone I love and trust. I kept thinking as the girls talked that I should pull Soeur Noble to the side, but just when I thought that, Soeur Sally got up and came and sat beside me. She gave me a hug and I was fighting to keep the tears from coming. Then she asked if there was something she could do for me and I told her yes, I would like to talk to her. We went into the other room and I told her about how I was really tired and wanted to talk to President Woolley. I poured out my soul to her and … to me, it was an answer to my prayer to have Soeur Noble and Soeur Sally show up that night.

I went to bed with a prayer in my heart. It was another stressful night physically. I was having pain and I couldn't sleep well, although I was very tired. I had a dream, or half-dream, that night (since I couldn't sleep well). My body was aching and in my dream I saw Soeur Milly, who was helping me get past the pain. She kept talking and she was just there while Soeur Howard was somewhere behind me. Each time I looked at Soeur Milly and she spoke to me, the pain would go away. When I looked at Soeur Howard, who was distracting Soeur Milly, the pain would come back. I remember encouraging Soeur Milly not to listen to Soeur Howard but to continue to do what she was doing; continue to be herself. "You help me when you are who you are." That was my dream.

I woke up Sunday morning and was very tired, and I didn't want to get out of bed. I didn't want to go to church. But I reminded myself that I was a missionary and that I had to get up and go. Well, we got up and caught the bus to church. I remember thinking I have no idea what the Lord wants me to do, but I'll try to do my best whatever task is given to me.

We got to the church and it went okay, at least for the first hour. Then I had to go teach the Gospel Principle class that started 30 minutes late. It was hard for me to stand up there and teach. The French didn't come as easily and my mind went blank. I was exhausted and confused. It was hard. I was really struggling emotionally and mentally. I thought about how I just couldn't continue on with the mission work like this. I just couldn't! So at the end of Relief Society, I saw Soeur Noble and a thought came to me, *Go to Soeur Noble, she is there.* But I didn't want to leave my companions. Then Soeur Milly said, "There goes Soeur Noble." It was as if she was giving me my queue, and I couldn't wait any longer. I told Soeur Milly and Soeur Howard to go ahead into the chapel and I would be okay for a minute. I had to go see Soeur Noble.

Soeur Howard didn't want to let me go, but I pleaded with her to just leave me alone. I walked off towards Soeur Noble. The closer I got, the harder it was for me to hold my tears back. I just walked straight into the arms of Soeur Noble and the tears came and I couldn't stop crying. Soeur Noble put me into the car and asked me what was wrong. I just explained to her that I couldn't do it anymore. I couldn't do the missionary work the way it was expected of me.

To make a long story short, we found Elder Zane, and Soeur Noble asked him if I could stay here in PK7 with her and Soeur Sally until President Woolley called me. He said yes. So here I am in PK7 with the same two companions that I left a week ago. Soeur Milly took it hard. She didn't want to be Sister Howard's companion anymore. She cried and cried. We encouraged her. We told her to talk to Elder Zane and ask for a transfer. Soeur Sally spoke to Soeur Howard alone and told her to speak to her companion and work with her.

Last night I came here to PK7, and at about 8:00 p.m. President Woolley called me. It was amazing to me that he called back so soon. I spoke to him about my health and told him that I was ready to go home. He agreed with me. He told me that he thinks I'm making a wise decision and he told me that he would speak to Doctor Nielsen (the mission doctor) tomorrow.

Today, Soeur Noble called Doctor Nielsen in Australia and he told her that he spoke to President Woolley and told him that I should go home to get better care. He also said that President Woolley would be calling the area presidency to put in my request to go home.

So those are the current events. I just want to say that I know that God loves me. I know that He loves me. I know that He sees me and He is constantly there. I love Him. I know that I've made the right decision, but there are so many more decisions to be made and I have fear of making them. I have no idea where I will go and how I will go. I have no idea what I will do and how I will do. I know nothing except getting off the plane in Las Vegas. I want to make the right choice. I don't want to fail the Lord. I don't know exactly what He wants me to do. I have no idea! But I am *toujours* (always) praying! I love these Scriptures that Soeur Noble showed me yesterday.

Verily I say unto you my friends, fear not, let your hearts be comforted; yea, rejoice evermore, and in everything give thanks;

Waiting patiently on the Lord, for your prayers have entered into the ears of the Lord of Sabaoth, and are recorded with this seal and testament—the Lord hath sworn and decreed that they shall be granted.

Therefore, he giveth this promise unto you, with an immutable covenant that they shall be fulfilled; and all things wherewith you have been afflicted shall work together for your good, and to my name's glory, saith the Lord.

—Doctrine and Covenants 98:1-3

October 21, 2003 (Edited)

Time is very important, and my time has come!

I just want to express how blessed I am. How blessed I've been since coming on a mission. I had an opportunity to work side by side with the Lord and the Holy Spirit. I have seen things that not many get to see. I am so blessed. I was scared when I came on this mission. I didn't know what to expect or what the future would bring. He knows my concerns. He knows my situation and He is mindful of me. I know that I'm not all alone and I'm grateful that I can always pray and I will be heard and answered. I have read Scriptures where the Lord has promised if you ask, ye shall receive. If ye have faith, you can move mountains. If you listen to His voice, He will guide you and you will not have any worries. I testify that these Scriptures are true.

Time has been very important to me since coming on my mission, and now that I am leaving early, I'm excited to know what the Lord has planned for me next. I have no idea what's going to happen except that I'm going to continue to do what I know how to do; pray, read my Scriptures, and be obedient. I'm excited to go to the temple to be reminded of my covenants and to just go and sit and think about all the experiences that I've had this year! It has been an experience!

October 23, 2003 (Edited)

Heavenly Father is an amazing Father and I adore Him. I love Him. He is amazing! He has blessed me so much. He has walked with me, and even when I thought He was far away from me, He was still there. I love that Scripture that says: "After much tribulation, come the blessings." (Doctrine and Covenants 103:12). That is so true. I know that if I continue in faith and prayer and do all that has been commanded of me, I will be able to fulfill my callings here on this Earth and I will be able to obtain my eternal goal, which is eternal Life. I love my Savior and I'm grateful that I had the opportunity to speak about Him 24/7. What a privilege. Really, what a privileged! I love being a missionary and I'm sad to be released from this special calling, but I have hopes that the Lord has greater callings for me.

I know that the church is true, but that's not all. I know that one cannot have eternal joy until they learn who their Father is and trust in God that He will bless them and take care of them. I love the Gospel of Jesus Christ. I know my Father is toujours la! (Always there!) He is always there and He will be there when times get tough. He will not let me fail and I will not fail Him! He said in my patriarchal blessing that He has no intentions of me failing. He trusts me, and I trust and love Him. I say these things in the name of Jesus Christ, my Lord, my Savior, my Rock. Amen!

A Calling within a Calling

November 1, 2003 (Edited)

I just returned home from my mission, Fiji Suva Mission, Noumea New Caledonia. At first I didn't realize how seriously sick I was until each day that passed I started to feel a change in my body and in my daily routines. I know now that I'm really sick, but I will not let my sickness stop me from doing what I like to do best, and that's teaching the fullness of the Gospel. I don't know how much time I'll have on this earth, but I plan to use every moment wisely. I don't know what the future holds for me; however, I do know that I don't have any fear of dying. I know what awaits me and I have always been excited to see what's happening on the other side of the veil.

I know the Lord has a special work for me. I am excited to fulfill all my callings. When the doctors told me that this disease has no cure and that many die from it, the only thing I could think of is I must get busy. I must not waste any more time that the Lord has given me. This life is only temporary. We were never put here to stay here, but only to prepare for the next life. I don't have a fear of dying. I just have fear of not doing all that I'm supposed to … of using my time wisely. I know I'll see each of my loved ones again, for this is not the end, it's just the beginning. I have a lot of good things to look forward to. I know that God has a special plan for my life. I'm excited to have these experiences.

It seems as if everyone has been worrying about where my faith stands as far as knowing that I have this sickness. Everyone who has called me in my family has been encouraging me to have faith. They must not understand how much love I have for the Lord and how I know that this life is only temporary. I don't live to receive the blessings and happiness of just today, but I live to obtain the eternal gift that comes after this life. I know this life is temporary and it's a time that is given to us to prepare to meet God. The Lord gives us situations, then

He sees how we'll choose to handle it. He never leaves us alone to do it by ourselves.

I know that God is there, and this illness is a part of my life. Yes, I will probably have some bad days as much as good days, but I will not take my eyes off my eternal goal. I just need to endure for a little while, then I'll be able to rest from my afflictions. My faith in the Savior is always strong because I love Him and I know that He loves me! I love the Gospel plan. I love the Lord Jesus Christ. He is my Savior, and I know that the church of Jesus Christ of Latter Day Saints is the Lord's true church, even the church that has the authority to perform mighty miracles. I know this Gospel is true and I'm thankful to have it in my life. This is my testimony that I leave in the name of Jesus Christ, Amen!

Chapter 5

MY TRIAL, MY TESTIMONY OF THE MATTER

There is a story in the Holy Bible that is another one of my favorites. This is because I know that this story relates to me too, especially dealing with a hereditary disease like Lupus. It's the story about the blind man that the Savior healed by rubbing clay onto his eyes. This miracle is recorded in John chapter 9.

As the Savior was passing by, He saw a man who was born blind. His disciples asked Him in so many words whose fault was it that this man was born blind, his parents or himself. The Savior answered and said neither, "but that the works of God should be made manifest in him." (John 9:3). Basically, what I get from the Lord's answer is that it was the will of the Lord that this man was born blind that he may be an instrument in God's hands when the time came. As you read on, you'll see that many miracles came from this one event of the Lord healing the blind man. Not only was the man healed by the Savior, but many came to know about the Lord because of it.

I'm sure the blind man had many trials before being healed by the Savior. He was a beggar, as the Scriptures put it. So, yes, life hasn't always been easy for him; but little did he know, and many others, for that matter, that he played a very important part in the Lord's plan. We all do. We all have a part in the plan of salvation. As we learn and become closer to the Lord, He willingly shows us our part.

Never get discouraged when life seems to be going left on you instead of right. Just trust in the Lord and ask for His divine help. He will help! He will not only help you in your trials, but bless many others because of your triumph over your trials. The Lord will use you and your testimony to bring many to Him so that He can bless them as well. Being an instrument in the Lord's hands is a privilege, an honor, and a joy. First we have to allow Him to help us get to that point.

This illness has definitely been a trial to me in so many ways. I won't even pretend like I enjoyed any of the pains that came with the flare-ups. This has been a learning process for me. Over the years, I have experienced many nights and mornings in tears because of the pain or the depression that comes with this disease. Dealing with the change of my appearance that came from the side effects of the medications has been hard, and is still hard. I do try to remember the moments the Lord has blessed me or answered my prayers. I continually trust in Him to help me get through the tough times and thank Him when the good times are here.

One of my biggest trials, and something I had to learn, was to trust the doctors' judgment calls when it came to the medications. Month after month, I would say even years, the doctors would prescribe medications to help keep this Lupus in remission; but I felt that I knew my body more than they did, and didn't need as high a dosage of certain medications. I learned the hard way that when I took control of my own treatment and weaned myself off medications without the doctor's knowledge, it only caused me pain and a longer stay in the hospital. The following are journal entries of my encounters with doctors and trying to take matters into my own hands.

March 21, 2004 (Edited)

I went to the doctor earlier this week and he said I was doing well. He increased my dosage of CellCept and kept me on the same amount of prednisone. I felt disappointed, yet he told me I was doing well. A couple of days before my doctor's appointment, I went and bought some clothes because I didn't have any that fit. I am in a size 15-16 now when I used to be size 8. I was really discouraged, and hoping the doctor would hurry and get me off this prednisone. Well, he didn't even lower it like usual.

After stressing and worrying and praying about how and why I should go out and buy more medication when I felt like it wasn't even worth it, it finally came to me how much I need it. I just felt this calm feeling, and knew in my heart that I need it. I don't understand why or how, but the Lord knows more than me. So I decided I will do whatever I can to continue with the medication the doctor gave me, even if it does make me gain weight rapidly.

This morning I woke up physically sore and discouraged and didn't want to go to church, but I pushed myself and I'm so grateful I went.

I don't know what trials I'll have with this illness; I don't know what it's going to teach me. I do know that I'm grateful to have a patriarchal blessing like mine that promises me I will still be able to be in the service of God despite my physical trials. I don't want to have physical trials; but I know the Lord never gives us more than we can bear. I know I'm supposed to and will learn something while going through this illness. I know the Lord will be there for me. I do want to share one more thought about my health.

I had a couple of people in the ward try to tell me about herbal medicine instead of drugs. They said it would help my body more. I was very hesitant at first because I personally thought that medical doctors know more, and that my best option would be to follow their orders instead of a doctor who works with natural herbs. Lately I've been thinking twice about that. I've even been thinking about going and seeing a different doctor because I don't feel like my doctor really does his best with me. I don't know for sure what I should do. I just know that I want to help myself get better, and not just get better in one area while I'm getting worse in another. I'm not quick to take these natural medicines yet because I don't know how my body will react to them, especially if I'm on some heavy drugs right now. I just need to do more research for my own benefit.

I love my Heavenly Father. I know He is there for me. I know that He loves me and He will bless me with my needs as long as I continue to do my part. I must continue in prayer and read; and not just read, but search and study the Scriptures that I may find answers to my prayers. I know I must keep the commandments. If I do this, and remember to always serve the Lord, then I know He will always be there, especially when I feel no one else is. I know the Gospel is true and this is my testimony in the name of Jesus Christ, Amen!

April 23, 2004 (Edited)

For the last month I haven't been taking my medications right, and especially this past week. I've just been in an "I don't care" mood, or "I'm tired of taking these pills in order to do what I want" mood. So, I haven't been taking my pills like I should have. I've been feeling the results of it. I do want to get better, and the last time I went to the doctor he showed me my lab work and I could see that I was improving. I love my Lord and Savior and I love the Gospel, for it is what keeps me going, and I say this in Jesus' name, Amen!

May 4, 2004 (Edited)

This morning I woke up feeling much better physically, mentally, emotionally, and spiritually. Last night I was so tired I was breaking myself down. I cried and cried until I had a very bad headache and couldn't cry anymore. I didn't go to work today because I really wanted to go to the temple and I didn't want to wait until after work when I would be too tired to go. I hesitated to stay home from work because I know that Tammi (my roommate) would be here and I don't want to be around anyone right now. I feel like whenever I'm around others, I do something to make them mad or they do something to make me mad. I don't want to be ugly towards people. Sometimes I feel like I can't control my attitude or moods; that's why I try to stay away.

This morning, Tammi suggested that I should ask the doctor for another type of medicine that would counteract the side effects of my other medicines, such as discouragement and depression. I don't want to be on any more drugs than I am already on. I lowered my prednisone pills from 30mg to 20mg. The past three days I really felt the consequences of that. So I decided the next time I go down on them, I'm going to take it 5mg less at a time. Man, there was one point when I couldn't get up off the floor because I was in so much pain. I hate drugs. I hate the fact that I have to take these medications in order to keep going.

May 16, 2004 (Edited)

Okay, so two days ago I went to the doctor and at first I was scared to even mention that I lowered my medicine, but I asked the Lord to be with me. I told the doctor the truth and he was mad at me at first, but of course he got over it because it's not his body. He lowered my prednisone some more. Now I'm on 15mg of prednisone, which is good for me, but I have to increase the CellCept. I'm okay with that.

I told the doctor that I wouldn't bother with my medicine anymore, but I'm not so sure about that. I have no intentions of bothering with it before I go see him again; however, if he doesn't get me off this stuff by August, I will get myself off. I do want to be obedient, but I don't want the doctors using me as an experiment.

Today I had to sit down and ask myself, what can I learn from this situation? I became sick and have to rely on medication for my body to function the way I want it to. Why did the Lord give me this type of calling/trial? How and what can this illness teach me? I don't know! I honestly can't answer that question with a satisfying answer right now.

I just know that I must go on by continuing to trust in the Lord and have hope. I say this in Jesus' name, Amen!

April 6, 2005 (Edited)

I've had some physical trials since I last wrote in this journal, and I have overcome them. Today I went to the doctor for my regular 2-month check-up and you know … well, just let me say that no doctor can heal me. They don't even have the slightest clue. All they can do is prescribe drugs for the pain and basically that's it.

For the past year I've been going to see the doctor and the maximum time I would spend in his office is 10 minutes, if that. I shouldn't complain because I know they must be doing the best they can. I'm just frustrated because to them it's okay if I'm on all these pills and I really don't want to be. I'm trying to keep my promise that I made to friends and family and myself that I will take the medication the doctor gives me and won't lie to them anymore. I'm back on 5mg of steroids and after losing 20 pounds I gained 7 more back. I hate it, but I'm trying to do what I'm supposed to. I'm working on it. I guess I don't know as much as I thought, either.

August 7, 2005 (Edited)

I got out of the hospital two days ago after being there for six days. On Wednesday, I started feeling pain on the right side of my neck. This wasn't the first time I'd felt it; therefore, I thought the pain would wear off soon enough. Thursday it got worse, and Friday it was just unbearable. I couldn't focus at work. So right after work, I went to the clinic. The medicine that was prescribed to me didn't work all that well because both Friday and Saturday night was like HELL!

By early Sunday morning I woke up Tammi and had her take me to the urgent care. My whole neck had swollen by then and I couldn't swallow or breathe. After five hours at the urgent care, they gave me morphine and called the ambulance to come and get me. They said that I had a blood clot in my artery on the right side of my neck. By the time I got to the hospital, everyone was attending to me. They said they might have to do surgery right away because the blood clot could break off into my lungs or my brain and both could cause death immediately. As I lay there in pain listening to all of this, I just felt like this was all a dream or nightmare.

After a few days, the doctors didn't want to do surgery, but instead decided to try to control the clot in a more careful way. They put me on blood thinners, which are pills I might have to take for the rest of my life. They also raised my dosage of prednisone to 40mg again. I have to get shots in my stomach twice a day until my blood level is normal again. I called my momma right away and sent for her from Chicago. So my momma is here with me right now and she is a huge blessing to me.

I don't understand everything. I don't understand why some things happen the way they do. I do know that all I need to understand is to trust in the Lord no matter what and know that He is! God loves me and I know He has a plan for my life. I have no idea what this plan consists of except that at the end, I know I'll be happy.

I love my family I'm glad my momma came without any hesitation. I love my Heavenly Father and I've never been afraid of death so I don't want to start now. I just want to be prepared and have peace and comfort through it all. That's all I ask for. I close now in Jesus' name, Amen.

August 15, 2005 (Edited)

I have no clue where I should start. Oh my goodness, so much has happened since I last wrote in this journal. So many miracles have been seen; so many lessons have been taught and learned. I really don't know where to start.

I went to see my rheumatologist, who has been my doctor for the last couple of years. He just looked as if he had no clue how to help me, which is fine. I'd rather he say, "I don't know," than guess and experiment on me.

On Friday I went to see my primary doctor, and as I sat in her office she explained everything to me. She looked at me and said, "Keela, you are lucky; you should have died. In my lifetime of practicing, I've only seen two people with blood clots, but none ever where you have it, or anyone as young as you." I was amazed. When I was in the hospital, all I was concerned about was the pain. I didn't care how dangerous it was; that didn't bother me. But when Doc told me that I should have died, it made me think of how God is with me.

I went to get my blood drawn and the nurses were also amazed at my condition. Let me just say that … this is very sacred to me … very sacred … but I felt like people looked at me as if I was an angel. I mean, when I walked past people or when they came to assist me, they looked at me with amazement, with respect, with honor or something. You could see it in their eyes … they wanted to do their best to help. And everything fell in order from blood exams to x-rays to doctor visits. I didn't feel angelic, but that is how I was treated. My momma said, "Keela is blessed. She is a miracle and everyone around her will be blessed." It was a very beautiful and nice thing to say.

The doctors in the hospital said that they'd never seen anything like this. There was one particular doctor, a nose, ear, and throat doctor, who came into my room at the hospital. He looked at the CT scan results with the blood clot, then he looked at me, and then again at the CT scan results, and back at me. He shook his head and said, "I've never seen anything like this. I've only seen this with someone who was shooting drugs in their neck." Tammi, who was in the room with me, laughed. She knew better than anybody that would never be the case with me, knowing how much I hated even taking my prescription drugs with a passion. But the doctor just stood there in amazement.

My primary doctor helped me understand why that doctor looked or stared with amazement. She helped me understand why everyone was going crazy at the hospital. It was because in her words, "You should have died." This is a miracle. God has spared my life, and I don't need to ask why. He prepared me for this a long time ago.

When I first got sick and I knelt down that night before I went to the hospital in Fiji, I knew it was part of God's plan. Although I was in pain I said, "Not my will, Lord, but thy will be done. Just give me the strength to get through it." I felt comfort. I felt His Spirit. The same thing happened with this last experience. The night before I went to the hospital, I knelt down and said the same thing and felt the same Spirit. It's like the Lord prepares me before I go into the hospital for something like this. He prepares me with peace and comfort.

Saturday I went to the temple and that was a good experience. I got a lot of peace and comfort from going there.

On Sunday I went to church, and it was wonderful. After church, I got a blessing from my home teacher. That experience was amazing. I barely even knew this guy. I met him and we talked for like five minutes. I explained the situation about my health. As we were introducing ourselves, I told him that I had served on a mission in Fiji. Well, come to find out, President Woolley, who was my mission president, was my home teacher's patriarch. My home teacher grew up in the same ward as President Woolley. After talking a little about my mission and health, my home teacher and another priesthood holder who was with him anointed my head with oil and gave me a blessing. The blessing was what I needed to hear from my Heavenly Father at this time of my life. My home teacher gave the blessing and he spoke with power from God, having the authority to do so.

It was beautiful. And what was so beautiful about it was that I knew it was from my Heavenly Father. I knew God was speaking to me through my home teacher. My home teacher didn't know anything about my family, didn't know anything about my week, with my trials and how I didn't complain to God; yet these things were mentioned in the blessing. Like I've said many times before, I don't know the exact plan that Heavenly Father has for my life. I do know that I love being an instrument in His hands. I told Tammi that if I can see miracles in my life every day like I have these past two weeks, I don't want to be cured. I mean it. The Gospel is great! I love it with all my heart. I love it. It's a great work and I love being involved.

Chapter 6

BE STILL, MY SOUL

Nevertheless the Lord seeth fit to chasten his people;
yea, he trieth their patience and their faith.
Nevertheless--- whosoever putteth his trust in him
the same shall be lifted up at the last day ...
—Mosiah 23:21-22

There will be times in life when you will be doing all that you're supposed to be doing and all that you know how to do as far as keeping the Lord's commandments. Life might seem peaceful and too good to be true. Then just when you least expect it, something happens that causes great disappointment or even heartbreak; something that will definitely put your faith in God to the test. This actually will happen a lot in life; at least for mine it has.

The key is not to lose that hope or faith no matter the outcome, no matter what! Remember, this life is a test and is full of experiences that are to help us to become like Heavenly Father. He is perfect and keeps His promises. Our timing may not be His timing. There are different levels and different types of faith; still, the Lord promised that if we have faith as a grain of mustard seed, we could move mountains (Matthew 17:20). How powerful is that? We also have to remember that it's all according to the Lord's will, for He sees it all. He sees the whole picture when we can only see what is in front of us, and sometimes that's not anything at all until we take that leap of faith.

Sarah, in the Old Testament, waited patiently and obediently to be blessed with a child. Abraham, though he had children, already wanted nothing more than to have a child with Sarah. They were promised and given a son, whom they named Isaac. Then Abraham was commanded to sacrifice Isaac. Without hesitation, Abraham was willing and ready to keep the commandment and follow the will of the Lord … until the angel stopped him. This was indeed to test Abraham's faith and obedience in the Lord.

I was very young and immature in my first years of dealing with this disease. As I've gone through the trials, I've learned certain things that I needed to change about myself, and also what I needed to appreciate more in life. I was and still am a very stubborn person, and sometimes can be prideful. But I'm learning like everyone else, just in a different way. This illness has taught me a lot of patience and has strengthened my faith in the Lord and His plan for me.

At the end of 2005, I met a handsome young man who I thought was the love of my life. We were married in 2006 in the Las Vegas LDS Temple. This marriage eventually resulted in a divorce, but there are trials that I had with my illness while married that not only tested my faith in God, but helped me to understand the Lord and His plan for me a little better, though I couldn't see the whole picture.

September 8, 2006 (Edited)

Yesterday, I went to the doctor to see if I can have children. The OB-GYN was straightforward and honest with me. He didn't hide anything that he wanted to say. He came straight in and shook my hand with a smile then got down to business.

He said that I couldn't have children. He said that with the history of my blood clot and kidney damage and me being on the type of medication that I'm on, I can kill myself. He said that my health is in no condition to have babies and that I'm not a good candidate to be a mommy. I was shocked and hurt … very hurt and disappointed. I was angry with the doctor for telling me that. He didn't know me; he'd never even met me. Then he explained to me that there wasn't any type of birth control I could really use because of my health. I was a little happy that I didn't have to start taking something else that I didn't agree with.

As I was leaving his office he apologized for being so bold, but he wanted to stress to me how important it was for me not to get pregnant again. (I'd had a miscarriage a week or two before this doctor visit.)

So many people have been telling me, "Keela, don't get pregnant. You don't want to get pregnant, Keela. Don't do it. You can't do it." I never thought they were right. I always had it in my mind that I was going to be okay. Heavenly Father was going to perform another miracle just like He did with the blood clot. But now hearing the doctor who had a little bit more knowledge than my family telling me this, it made me sad … very sad.

I always thought and felt like there were children waiting for me. Waiting for me to make all the right choices so that they could come down and be with me. Although I felt so hurt and torn inside, I also knew that I couldn't complain. It's just hard not to think about it and hurt; but I'll get through it. I will!

June 7, 2007 (Edited)

I was just told by my husband that he wants a divorce. We were going through some hard times so we separated. I was hurt, very hurt. I went to work and I felt sick and dizzy. People were telling me I was pregnant. I didn't believe them because I didn't think I could get pregnant since the miscarriage happened.

I was two weeks late with my period, so I decided to go on my lunch break to get an EPT, just in case I might be. I didn't want to lose this baby if I was. In my mind I was telling myself that it was impossible to be pregnant. Besides, Heavenly Father wouldn't give me a child during a time like this.

I took the test in the bathroom and as I was waiting for the results, I was going back and forth about how I hoped I was and how I hoped I wasn't. I grabbed the test and sure enough, it was positive. I was shocked. I was so shocked that I wasn't excited for a while. I didn't understand. This couldn't be, not right now.

As days went by I made an appointment with an OB-GYN. They did a urine test and it was confirmed that I was pregnant. To me, it was a miracle. Yes, a miracle. Since then I have been seeing two OB-GYNs. Every two weeks I'm in one or the other's office. One is a specialist because of the Lupus.

I have to take blood thinners again, but this time I'm doing it by needle shots in my stomach only. The doctors are afraid of me getting another blood clot because babies make your blood thick. I have to give my own self the shots every day.

How has it been being pregnant? Well, I'm three and a half months right now and the baby is still doing good. When I went to go get my first ultrasound I was in tears. I couldn't feel the baby move yet but when I saw it, it was amazing, and I felt the angels around me. I'm grateful to be pregnant. It has its downfalls; I can't sleep comfortably at night. I always have to go to the restroom every hour, etc. But I'm very happy to know that this baby is alive and will be mine. My husband and I are still separated and I don't know what the future will bring. I just know that I have a baby to look after now.

The Lord is placing the baby in my care and it's my responsibility to teach him about his Heavenly Father. I know it's a boy. It has been revealed to me numerous times and that's what I want; to raise a missionary, a worthy priesthood holder, a willing servant of the Lord.

This has been really hard on my body, and I don't think I will have another child biologically. If so, it will be in a very long time. My due date is supposed to be November 28, 2007. I think it will be sooner than that. Heavenly Father is a God of miracles and He has proven that with me yet another time. It all starts with faith. I love my Savior and am thankful for the Gospel plan. I say this in Jesus' name, Amen!

June 19, 2007 (Edited)

How am I doing? Well, I'm trying to hang in there. Mornings are really hard for me. When I get up in the morning to start my day, my body just doesn't want to move. I feel like a truck just hit me about five times. My muscles are so sore, along with my ever-growing breasts. And my body just feels too heavy for me to lift out of bed or anywhere. The last time I weighed myself was last Wednesday at the doctor's office. I weighed 177 pounds then. Physically, it's been hard and exhausting. I have my emotional problems on top of it. So basically, when I come home I go right to bed.

I worry about how the baby is doing every day because I don't feel it much and when I do, I'm not sure if it's the baby or not. My body is so tired and I honestly don't feel like I'll have another child by birth for at least five years, if ever. It's just hard on my body. I do have to close by saying that I'm grateful I'm able to have this child. What a blessing this child will be to me. What a miracle! I'm thankful for the

Gospel. I'm thankful for God, and pray and hope that He will always be mindful of me with His love, and I say this in Jesus' name. Amen.

August 2, 2007 (Edited)

On July 11, 2007, I went to my regular doctor's appointment with the OB-GYN. During the check-up, the doctor mentioned that she was worried I have pre-eclampsia. Pre-eclampsia is a pregnancy disease that causes high blood pressure, swelling, excessive weight gain, and can stop the blood flow to the placenta and kill the baby and sometimes the mom, too. She told me that she wanted me to do some tests and see me again in a week. If I really had pre-eclampsia, she would have to stop me from working until after the baby is born. She wanted to put me on bed rest. So we checked for the baby's heartbeat and he was still doing well.

I left the doctor's office unable to give them a drop of urine because I really couldn't go. I went to the temple and did a session. I was happy. BUT … I was stressing. I was sad about my marriage and I was stressing and worrying when I shouldn't have been.

Saturday came three days from the doctor's visit and I had a cousin come into town to visit. I didn't rest like the doctor told me to do. I didn't get to bed until after 3:00 a.m., which is not good with my health conditions. The same day my engine light came on so that caused more worries for me.

By Sunday the car really wasn't running right and I knew I couldn't take it to work. The first person I tried to call to help me out was my husband (we were still separated). He wasn't there. When he didn't answer his phone, or wasn't home, that only stressed me out more and my blood pressure, I'm sure, was sky high.

Monday came and my brother's girlfriend, my niece's mom, was the one who had to take me to work. That morning when I woke up the phone rang and I didn't want to answer it. My momma tried to come and talk to me and I didn't want to talk to her. When I opened my eyes that morning I was really, really sad. I didn't feel life. I got out of bed to say my prayers and my body felt different. I started to worry a little. I looked in the mirror; there was something different about my body. I thought to myself, *There is something wrong with the baby.* I didn't feel him, spiritually. It wasn't too often that I felt him physically, but I knew that he was there. This Monday morning was different.

Work and the people around me were stressing me out. I wanted to be alone. I went to the restroom and cried. I prayed and I cried because I felt overwhelmed. I couldn't see any sunlight in my life. I prayed and asked God to help me see the sunlight and take the storms away.

I went back to my desk and maybe 15 to 20 minutes later I got a call on my cell phone, it was one of my OB-GYNs. She told me to get to the hospital now. She was very calm but made it sound like something I should be concerned about. I asked her questions but she only told me to get to the hospital, her partner was waiting for me to arrive. I told her that I was at work, and she told me this couldn't wait and I needed to leave work. Okay, now I knew it was serious. So I promised her that I would go immediately.

Once I hung up the phone I started to panic. I just couldn't hold back the tears because I knew now that there was something wrong with the baby. I told my manager that I had to go and he understood. My coworker volunteered to take me. I quickly called up my momma to let her know what the doctor said and she told me that she would meet me at the hospital. Five minutes later, my estranged husband called me to see what was going on. I guess my momma called him. I told him the story about the phone call and he agreed to meet me at the hospital.

I got to the hospital and settled in. They tried to check for the baby's heart … nothing. So they called the OB specialist that I'd been seeing. He came in with the ultrasound machine to see the actual picture of the baby. He rubbed the instrument onto my stomach and I looked at the machine. There was my baby boy, all balled up in a corner, no sign of life. The doctor turned to me and said, "Yeah, there's no heartbeat." I just couldn't believe it. I didn't want to believe it. I put my hands over my face and just started screaming out, "NO! NO! NO! NO!" and started crying. I remember my momma hugging me and telling me she was sorry.

The nurses surrounded me, trying to give comfort. The doctor then started to explain to me what happened. He said that I had pre-eclampsia that had developed into a disease called HELLP syndrome (Hemolysis, elevated liver enzymes, low platelet count). He said that the blood stopped flowing into the placenta and the baby died. He also told me that they called me into the hospital because whether the baby was alive or not, they would have to deliver it because I was slowly dying. With HELLP syndrome that meant my platelets were decreasing a great deal each day. He said that a normal person's platelets are at 150,000 at least; mine were at 24,000 and still decreasing. The only way to cure this disease is to deliver the baby as fast as possible. He also said by the baby only being 20 weeks there was no guarantee that he would make it after delivery. So the baby was bound to die in this situation; their job was to save the mother first. He told me that I was very sick. I might not look it or feel it, but I was really sick.

I had to deliver the baby. I didn't want to, but they had to remove him. I think if the baby didn't die and was still alive, I probably would have risked my life trying to save his by keeping him inside as long as I could. I don't know … but he was dead, so there was no point of keeping him inside. I had to be induced and delivered regular instead of any other way because the doctors were afraid I would either bleed to death, since I was on blood thinners, or get clots later. I was in the hospital for two days before the baby finally came. July 18, 2007, is when I delivered the baby, at 6:47 a.m. He came out breached, weighed 6 ounces and was 6 inches long. He was very small, but he had all his toes and fingers, and even his little pee-wee.

I don't understand a lot that has happened. Was it Heavenly Father's intention to not let this pregnancy go all the way out? I don't know. I do know that I was pregnant, which was a miracle for me, and I do know that the baby was alive at one point. He was mine; he is mine. I just pray that the Lord will continue to bless me and hopefully one day I will be able to have children, whether by adoption or by other ways. I was grateful for the experience. I will not forget it, neither will I forget Baby Wilson, he is real to me.

Two weeks before all of this happened, I received a priesthood blessing from the missionaries. It was another one of those special blessings when Heavenly Father was very detailed with me. In the blessing he told me to: "Be still, Heavenly Father has His hands in the situation, everything will work out."

All I can do is trust in His will and stay faithful. No one knows how much I desire to be a mother more than God Himself. I know that someday I'll have that opportunity, whether in this life or the next.

August 4, 2007 (Edited)

The OB specialist explained to me that the doctor that visited with me a couple of days ago is a blood specialist, also known as a hematologist. The hematologist was thinking that my disease that is called HELLP syndrome was turning into TTP (Thrombotic Thrombocytopenic Purpura), which is basically the same thing. But the only way to cure TTP is by having a plasma transfusion. The OB then told me that he told the hematologist he didn't think I needed that. So they were waiting a few days to see if my platelet count would go up since I delivered the baby.

After the baby was delivered, they moved me to the maternity recovery room. I was there for two days before Doctor F., the hematologist, showed up again. I didn't like this doctor because he was being very pushy about getting the plasma transfusion. He told me that if I didn't do it, I would eventually die. My platelets were really low and I needed them to stop me from bleeding or else I could bleed to death. He explained that without high platelets I would suffer brain and kidney damage and eventually die. I understood what he was saying but I didn't want a tube in my neck. I was scared.

I finally agreed to go through with the procedure. I was moved to a regular medical floor because it had nothing to do with maternity anymore. Sunday, July 22, 2007, they did a small surgery on my neck, placing a port with tubes in a main vein that would help complete the transfusion. For eight days I had this treatment, and it wasn't as bad as I thought. It was a little uncomfortable, but when the treatment started I was put to sleep with the Benadryl. They had to give me Benadryl in case I had an allergic reaction to the new plasma that was given to me. The treatment did work. My platelets started going up. I guess Doctor F. was right; he was still pushy. I was in the hospital for 15 days. I could've left a day earlier but my blood pressure kept going up and they wouldn't let me go. That was a trial of its own.

Being in the hospital this time was different than any other time for me. This time it was more of a trial. I guess because I didn't really feel sick or any pain. So in my mind I was thinking I was well, but internally I was really sick. It was an experience, and I have learned and seen a lot.

Chapter 7

STOP FIGHTING AND LISTEN!

*If all you know is what you see with your natural eyes and hear
with your natural ears, then you will not know very much.*
—*Elder Boyd K. Packer*

Have you ever prayed and asked God for help, and it felt like things were getting worse instead of seeing your prayers answered? I witnessed that many times, and a few that I will never forget. However, I must say that **God always answers!** It may not be in the form that we expect or in the time that we expect, but He always answers our prayer that is ended in Jesus Christ's name, who is our advocate with the Father.

This next experience that happened in 2008 lasted for six months and was my longest trial ever. I felt like God was ignoring me at times. In actuality, He was attending to me and answering my prayers, but I was fighting against His will and His helping hands.

God doesn't give us trials to punish us. He loves us. Many times our trials come from us creating them. Either way, trials will only teach us and help us to grow and become strong where we are weak. Sometimes when we pray and ask God for His help, we will probably see things getting worse before they get better because of several reasons. At least for me, I would say that one of those reasons is that He is trying to get my attention. I have a tendency to want to do things my own way, and God can't help me if I'm not listening to Him. Another reason is that He is working on something that is most likely beyond my comprehension at that moment and although I may not understand what He is doing, I just need to trust, listen, and follow His guidance. Easier said than done; I of all people know this fact.

Learning to sit still and let God help has always been a weakness for me. It's usually after I've caused a lot of damage that I realize I can't do it alone, I need His help after all.

After being in remission for a good year, the longest trial of my life yet was right around the corner. I know that things probably would've been different if I'd just trusted the doctor and followed his lead, but I refused to do things the way other people wanted me to. After all these years of living with Lupus and going through the trials that I'd already been through, I still hadn't realized how serious the matter was.

In my mind it was just another obstacle to slow me down and that I was going to get over eventually. I had to come to realize that it's not an obstacle I can get over alone, but I need the help of others. God answers our prayers and places certain people in our path to help us overcome trials. We are all learning together, but still He often answers our prayers by using someone else to help us. I don't know if I learned everything I was supposed to learn from this next trial but I did learn that I need to stop fighting, and listen. I did learn to let go and just let God do whatever He is doing, even if I don't understand or see what is going on.

I don't know if this trial helped anybody around me, but for me it did teach me humility and to trust God, who is all powerful, all merciful, unchangeable in His love, and a wonderful Heavenly Father who doesn't just give us what we want, but what is best for us.

November 20, 2008 (Edited)

For the past three months, I've been having a flare-up with my Lupus, mainly joint pains. I went to the doctor, my rheumatologist, to be exact, and he confirmed from the results of my blood tests that I was having a flare-up and that it didn't look good. He wanted to put me on steroids again. I'd been off that medication for a year. It wasn't because the doctor didn't want me on it, but I refused to be on it. He told me again that I need to take the steroids to help with my flare-ups.

Again I told him no, not until I am on my death bed. Well, instead, he doubled my dose of the CellCept, which I was okay with. After a couple of weeks I noticed the abnormal bruises and red marks on my arm. I knew something was happening, but I didn't want to believe it. A couple of days later, tired of feeling nauseas, and having headaches and dizzy spells every day, I decided to go online to see what information I could find about these marks on my body.

After 30 minutes of research, I knew what I had. I knew that I had TTP again; the same thing I'd had after losing the baby a year ago. I prepared myself for the hospital. I knew without a doubt that it was TTP, but I was hoping I was wrong.

I went to the urgent care and after waiting over two hours, they finally confirmed my assumptions that I had TTP. They called the ambulance, and had me admitted to the nearest hospital. The ER reconfirmed that I had TTP, but they also told me what was causing it; the CellCept. They immediately took me off of CellCept and put me back on 60mg of prednisone. Needless to say, I wasn't at all happy. I'd have to receive a plasma transfusion. I'm trying to stay positive. I didn't think I would be back here, but here I am. I'm not happy, but it's hard to be ungrateful knowing that God has been guiding me and blessing me. I love my Savior and I am ever so grateful for the Gospel. I say this in Jesus' name. Amen.

January 19, 2009 (Edited)

I'm still in the hospital. It's going on my third week. I do feel a little better than I did when all this started. Let me start from the beginning. The year 2008 started out wonderful for me. I went to St. Louis and Chicago in January to visit Grandma and help her sell her home that I grew up in. It was during the winter, so it was really cold in Chicago. I had a fear that I would get sick and have a flare-up with this Lupus, but I didn't. I did get sick with a cold and sore throat, but nothing I couldn't endure.

In February, I had a flare-up with my joints. By the summer I was better. My health was good to me, and I had the blessing and opportunity to spend quality, fun time with my family. My niece and nephews, Brianna, JR, and Andrew, spent the summer with us and I took them, along with Sariah and my mom, to Disneyland and the beach. We got on rollercoasters and I was able to enjoy the very freezing cold California beach water. It was fun, and my health was still good. I went to Utah to visit a friend and her family in August and was able to get on more scary rollercoasters. It was fun, but I knew I wasn't being fair to my body after all the time it was holding up for me.

By September I'd started to have joint pains, really bad joint pains, and headaches. I felt tired, more than normal.

By October, my fingers started to swell and become really sore. I couldn't bend them on some days. Then my wrists became inflamed and my shoulders; nevertheless, I didn't let that stop me from living my life. I had a visit with my rheumatologist by the end of October and he wanted to put me on Prednisone, but I refused (stubborn me). I think things would've been different for me today if I would've listened and taken the drugs again. Instead, he increased the dose of my CellCept. My headaches didn't go away, but rather increased. My tiredness increased and of course my stress level increased because I was in the process of buying a home, too. I'd decided by mid-November to take a day off from work to rest my body. I slept in and rested, then I felt a prompting to take this time off to go to the clinic. I knew something was wrong with me, but I was too tired to go to the doctor.

I noticed red pin-dots on my arm and a big purple bruise. I researched that on the Internet and ITP came up. As I read about it, it became clear to me that I had TTP, which is the same thing that caused me to lose the baby a year and a half ago. I decided to follow the prompting to go to the clinic. I went to the clinic that day and explained my concern. They did blood work and found that my platelets were at 19,000. They called the ambulance and had me rushed to the hospital. I think I was there for 2-3 days. They didn't give me a plasma transfusion, but a red blood cell transfusion and put me on 60mg of prednisone. That was hard to accept. I didn't want to do it, but it was a matter of life or death for me. They took me completely off of CellCept because the ER doctors thought it was causing my platelets to go down. They assigned me a hematologist and it happened to be the same doctor I'd had when I lost the baby, Doctor F. He is really good so I was happy to see him.

I left the hospital on 60mg of steroids and on iron pills. In just a week I had gained almost 10 pounds and my face had swollen up. I prayed every day and night that Heavenly Father would help me to be positive and help me to love myself.

I had a doctor visit with Doctor F. once a week and things were looking good. Then in a matter of one week, my platelets went from 75,000 to 56,000. Doctor F. told me that the prednisone wasn't working and he wanted to admit me into the hospital for a blood transfusion. That was hard news for me because I didn't have more time to take off from work and I had just bought a home. I needed to provide for myself. I was afraid and I just cried. I called my momma and Tammi and they both encouraged me that Heavenly Father will bless me. I said a prayer of my own asking Heavenly Father to help me to know what to do. I didn't want to lose my job or all that I had accomplished.

After praying about it, I asked the doctor if I could admit myself on Saturday instead of that day and he agreed. I went to the ER and waited six hours before getting seen by a doctor. They did blood tests on me and told me that my platelets were at 96,000. There was no need to do an emergency blood transfusion. They sent me home that same day, which made me happy. I returned to life as I knew it and continued to see my doctors.

My rheumatologist prescribed different pills for my Lupus and kidneys, along with keeping me on 20mg of prednisone. I was doing well; so I thought. Yes, I was big and gaining weight, losing my identity as I once knew it, but I was healthy. I didn't feel any pain.

On Christmas day, I wasn't my normal self. I knew something was wrong. That following weekend I went to the blood lab to get my weekly blood drawn for Doctor F.

Monday morning I was too tired to go to work but I went anyway. I had to because we were short-staffed and my job needed me to open the bank that day. I went and I was literally dragging myself. I was so weak it was hard for me to open a door. After two hours at work, my vision started to get blurry. I started to see double. People would speak to me or talk to me about something and I couldn't keep up with the conversation. I felt sick. I went to the restroom to lie on the floor. I cried a little and said a prayer to Heavenly Father. I then went to look at my cell phone and saw that I had a message. It was from Doctor F.'s office. I called him back and he told me that my platelets were at 7,000 and that was two days ago when I had my blood drawn. He told me to rush to the ER immediately.

I called my mom and told her the news and she told me that she would meet me there. I went to my boss and told him the news and he gave me permission to go. I slowly and dizzily walked to my car. I sat there for a good five minutes trying to figure out which hospital to go to. I could barely think to drive much less think of the directions.

I said a prayer and drove to the nearest hospital, which was three minutes away; one straight shot down the street. My chest started to hurt; I was short of breath, dizzy, and had a really bad headache. I went into the ER and they immediately did some tests on me. They told me that it seemed as if I was having a small heart attack, and my platelets were at 6,000. They were going to have me get a plasma transfusion and do a stress test on my heart. I was in that hospital for eight days before they released me. I left with a platelet count of 124,000, and I passed the stress test. I was okay.

The next day or night I was having high blood pressure problems. All I wanted to do was go to bed, but I got a severe headache that gave me the sign that my blood pressure was sky high. I got down on my knees and the more I prayed and pleaded with the Lord to take the pain away, the worse it got. I went downstairs and told my mom about my headache and she wanted to get my blood pressure. While she struggled with the machine, I decided to take another blood pressure pill, thinking it would help bring down my blood pressure. All the while this headache caused me to have shortness of breath and dizziness. I felt like someone had a hammer and was just beating me upside the head with it until I couldn't breathe anymore.

Finally my mom took my blood pressure and it was 215 over 134. My mom dropped the machine in fear. I told her to call 9-1-1. It felt like they took forever to get there but it was really within 5 to 7 minutes. By the time they got there my blood pressure was at 228 over something. It just kept going up and oh, I was feeling it. They took me to the hospital.

I'm really sick and this is where I need to be (in the hospital). It's a trial that I must go through, and He is with me to get through it. If God would've eased my headache or taken away my pain at home, I wouldn't have known that my platelets were going down again. I wouldn't have known what was causing the high blood pressure. I wouldn't have known that my kidneys were failing; I wouldn't have known the reality of my sickness. I needed to get to the hospital, and one way of getting me there in my stubbornness was feeling pain bad enough to go. At least that's how I see it.

God doesn't punish us or cause us to have afflictions. He will always be there to protect me and help me to get better. I guess I don't like to listen, so God has to allow certain things to happen in order to get my attention. It doesn't mean that He doesn't love me. As much as I hate staying long-term in the hospital, I know I need to be here. I'm not going to try to rush home anymore just to get back to work and the way of living. It's not worth the pain.

January 23, 2009 (Edited)

It's Friday and the 26th day in the hospital. My platelets on Sunday were 131,000. Then they went down to 103,000 on Monday. I was so discouraged and was reaching the end of my rope. I was losing hope for myself, but I said a prayer and with an encouraging family, I was able to just stick in there and not worry about the numbers of my platelets.

The doctor's goal is to get me to 200,000. It was time to do something different because obviously the plasma transfusion wasn't working for me anymore, and at this up and down rate, I was going to be in the hospital forever. So I remembered the doctors were telling me that the other option was chemotherapy or splenectomy. Neither one of them sounded good to me, but I pondered about it and prayed about it. I was leaning more toward chemotherapy because from my research on it, TTP wouldn't come back. I called Doctor F., the hematologist, and left a message for him to call me back with more information on chemotherapy.

A couple hours later, the hospital doctor came into my room and told me exactly what I was thinking earlier, that we need to go to Plan B. The plasma transfusion wasn't helping anymore. He said that a splenectomy seemed like it would be the next best step. I suggested the chemo. He then said that he will have Doctor F. come in to explain more about both options, and then I could decide.

Doctor F. came in that evening and when I saw him, I already knew what I wanted to do. I remembered some of the words of the priesthood blessing that I'd received last Sunday, "to listen to the doctors." Doctor F. stood and spoke with confidence and told me that he felt that a splenectomy would be best for me. He said that chemotherapy isn't guaranteed. He explained that if we did chemo, it would take 2 to 3 weeks before it would kick in and that I would have to be in the hospital during that time, whereas if they remove the spleen, which is where the platelets are going to be killed off, then it should help, and the results would show within 24 hours. I then asked him when can we start, and he said ASAP.

If my platelets go below 100,000 then we can't do it because I would bleed to death. That only made me think of how Heavenly Father was watching over me and had His hand involved with getting me well. My platelets wouldn't go up anymore because it's necessary to take care of the ultimate problem so that it wouldn't come down anymore; remove the spleen. My platelets also didn't go below 100 for the same reason. He was and is allowing it to stay above 100 so that the surgery and problem could be taken care of. Believe me, I've been praying and praying and praying that God would heal me and bless that my platelets would go up. My hope was that they would go up to 200,000 like the doctors wanted; but God knows all things. He heard and hears my prayers and He answers them in the best way that is good for me.

God knows best, and I just need to trust Him. It's hard when you can't see ahead, but God can. If I just take His hand and let Him be the leader, I know I can get through this. Normally, I would refuse the surgery because of fear and many other reasons, but because of those special words in that blessing, "Listen to the doctors," my heart has softened and I have become less stubborn. I'm ready, and I know that this end result will help me to become better. I put my trust in God and hope that all goes according to His will. I love the Lord and I say this in Jesus' name, Amen.

February 24, 2009 (Edited)

Here I am, back in the hospital. I had the splenectomy on January 26, 2009, and everything went well. I was sent home two days after the surgery. It took time, but I gained my strength back and got back into my routines. I had a platelet count of 564,000. It was a miracle, and made me happy. Then on Saturday morning, February 21, 2009, I got out the shower and saw red pin-dots on my arm. Oh, I knew very well what that meant. I went to the urgent care and sure enough, my platelets had dropped from 564,000 to 21,000 in three weeks. I was very bothered by that.

I went to the temple and it was good. It had been a very long time since I'd been to the temple. It was wonderful. I went to church on Sunday and felt good there, too. I was grateful to take the Sacrament worthily. All the while, this TTP was on my mind. I had prayed to God to take it away and allow my platelets to increase; "Not my will, but thy will be done," is how I concluded my prayer. I called my hematologist and I knew that I was going to go to the hospital. I actually wanted to; weird, but true. Doctor F.'s nurse told me to get to the ER. By the time I got to the ER my platelets had dropped to 15,000.

I don't know what all of this mean. I don't know why this is happening to me. I'm not even sure if I'm learning or understanding all of what God wants me to learn or understand. I just know that this is a trial … the longest trial ever. What will be the end result of the TTP? I don't know. I don't even think the doctors know. However, I believe in God and I know that He lives and loves me. He has always been there for me during tough and unsure times of my life. I know He is here with me today. I have a testimony of Jesus Christ and I know what He can do for me and all men. I will endure with Him being my strength. I won't and can't give up. This I know for sure. I do understand the plan of salvation, and this trying time will only make me stronger in faith and testimony. I love my Savior and say this in Jesus' name, Amen.

March 4, 2009 (Edited)

I've been trying to get back into the habit of reading my Scriptures every night because I need that strength. I need to feel my Father's love and heavenly presence.

I went to the hospital and I was there for eight days. I got out yesterday. My count was in the 300,000s yesterday and I was able to go back home. Today I had to go see Doctor F. so I can get permission to go back to work tomorrow. Well, things didn't work out like that. My counts dropped from 300,000 to 25,000 in one day. It was crazy. It was as if someone was stopping me from getting better and living my life. As soon as I leave the hospital, it drops. So now, the last resort is chemo.

Today, I got my first treatment of chemotherapy. I cried and cried, but I know that God is in control of my life. I see people, good people all around the world, doing good things in their lives and they are happy. Then I think of myself and for one moment I start to feel like things aren't fair for me, but I know … I know that I'm doing good things in my life, too. I know that God, all powerful, all knowing, all loving, and all merciful, sees and knows what is happening with me. I know that I am on His mind, in His thoughts, in His plan. No matter what happens, He will make sure I'm happy. I know I'm one of His priorities and He hasn't forgotten about me. I can't comprehend how I'm going to overcome this obstacle of TTP, but I know that I will. I know that I won't and can't let it defeat me. As long as I'm doing good things and listening and following the Holy Ghost, then the work will get done and I will fulfill all that God wants me to do. I love Him, and His love is what keeps me going. His love and the hope of eternal exaltation are what keeps me saying, "Okay, God, thy will be done." I know that Jesus lives and loves me. I know that the Gospel is true. I know that the Book of Mormon is true. I will be true to who I am, and that is a daughter of a powerful and loving God, my Heavenly Father. I say this in Jesus' name, Amen.

March 23, 2009 (Edited)

I am back in the hospital. I've been here for two weeks and guess what? I love it. Two Mondays ago Doctor F., my hematologist, called me and told me to go to the ER. My red blood cells were at 7.9 or something like that and my platelets were about 62,000. I knew I would be going back to the hospital, but I was tired. I went and stayed there at the hospital for six days, then got transferred to one where I can get the chemo treatment. I've been here for eight days now. This is the only hospital that does chemotherapy in Las Vegas. This Wednesday will be my third treatment. As I mentioned before, I'm so happy that I'm here at the hospital. I say that because here I had a chance to relax and just rest. I feel like I have no worries. I can just relax and let the Lord use me however He wants to use me. I feel good. I don't feel sick at all, although my blood shows differently. I just know I'm where I should be.

This TTP disease has been taking a toll on both my friends and family, but I see that they all have been drawing closer to the Lord through prayer and attending church. I have good nurses here with me. My momma and brother have been good to me. They usually come to visit once or twice a week. I know I'll get better and be able to enjoy life again, I just need to be patient. I have a desire to get married again and adopt many babies, but I also know that I have to be patient in that, too. I know that God sees me and knows what's best for me. I know that He will bless me as He always has. I feel at peace, relaxed, and happy. I'm not ready to go home yet. I want to stay here at the hospital until I know it's time to go home. The Gospel is true and I know that God lives. I say this in Jesus' name, Amen.

March 24, 2009 (Edited)

Right now I'm a little worried. I had another confrontation with one of the doctors yesterday and today my platelets went down. I am now at 282,000 platelets, when yesterday I was at 355,000. The doctor wanted me to do the chemo today and then get released. I told him that I didn't want to go home until I know for sure that I'm okay. He kept trying to tell me that I was okay because my platelets are above average. I told him of course they are, but they drop little by little every day and eventually they go below average. I told him I didn't want to get discharged only to come back tomorrow or three days later. He still wouldn't see my point and so to shut him up and get him out of my room I agreed to do the chemo today instead of Wednesday. It's like he doesn't care or have any interest in me getting better but is trying to push me out. I was so frustrated.

I had the chemo today and now I'm waiting on the doctor to come. I have a feeling that the doctor from yesterday is still going to want to let me go home, even though he sees that the TTP is still there. I think I'm going to have to go with my Plan B. I want to get a second opinion before going on a stronger dosage of chemo. To be honest, I'm just lost on what to do. I can't say that aloud because I don't want my family and friends to worry or be discouraged. I do feel lost and stressed-out. I don't think the doctors know what to do with me. It's all so frustrating.

April 3, 2009 (Edited)

On March 25, 2009, I came home from the hospital. That morning, which was a day after my third treatment of the chemo, my platelets went up by 30. I knew then that the end has come; I felt it. I didn't want to go home because I was so used to the hospitals. Home wasn't home for me. I had no routine, and didn't feel a purpose. I was lost and depressed for the first three days at home. Then I got down on my knees and prayed. I asked Heavenly Father to bless me with energy and strength and help me to be happy.

He answered my prayer right away. The next morning when I got up from bed, I felt like myself. I had energy, life, and a good spirit with me. I wanted to sing and dance to my favorite music. I started doing things I enjoyed doing. When I went back to the doctor, they told me that my platelets were still in the 300,000 range. Yep, the end of all this was here.

Today I'm back at the doctor's office to receive my last treatment of the chemo. I have arranged to go back to work next Wednesday. I'm actually looking forward to it. I have new goals in my life and I'm happy. I'm back to me again. This weekend is General Conference and I can hardly wait to hear what the speakers have prepared. Life is here again and I am happy to be able to enjoy it. I love my Savior and I say this in Jesus' name, Amen.

Chapter 8

AMAZING!!

It's no surprise to my friends and family how much I love and adore children. This next journal entry was one of the most joyous times of my life, despite the constant flare-ups. It was during the time that I was called by the bishop in my ward (area) to serve as the primary president, teaching the little children. I do believe that, just like my mission was a big part of the plan for my life, serving and teaching these children is included in that plan as well. It was one of the best times of my life yet.

March 24, 2013 (Edited)

I woke up this morning in tears because of the pain that I was feeling in my hands and wrists. I was so tired of hurting, especially when I wanted to do nothing more than serve the Lord. I said a prayer and the pain eased up. I went to church and got a priesthood blessing. My fingers and wrists still have a tingle to them, but I feel no pain. AMAZING! I love the Lord. I love that He blesses and heals me, for I know that He can. This whole day was a spiritual day for me. Sharing time with the children was the best. I gave the lesson, and anytime I speak of Jesus Christ I feel the Spirit so strongly, and I can feel the presence of the Lord.

My lesson was on Jesus Christ is our Savior. I had a few children tell Scripture stories about how people were saved, such as Alma the younger, ZeeZrom, and many more from the Bible and the Book of Mormon. My favorite part is when I didn't know what else to say after the Scripture stories, but I wanted the children to really understand how the Savior is present in their lives. So I took the picture of Jesus Christ and held it up in front of the children. I asked them very soberly how they feel when they see a picture of Jesus Christ. I had shy children raising their hand to tell how they felt. The Spirit was really strong. A four-year-old said that she feels good. A seven-year-old said that he feels the Holy Ghost. I said that I do, too (and I was near tears at this point). An eleven-year-old said that she feels God's love. A nine-year-old said that they can feel Heavenly Father near.

Oh my goodness, hearing the testimonies of these children brought me great joy. I bore my testimony of the Savior, and told the children how much He loves them and wants them to know Him. I encouraged them to learn about Him by reading the Scriptures and coming to church, and talking to Him in prayer. Oh, the Spirit was so strong!

A couple of fathers were in the back of the room. After primary, one father came to me (he was a visitor) and said that primary was great, and it made him want to move to this ward. That made me smile. The Lord knows how much I love these children. It doesn't matter if it's a child at the grocery store, a visitor of the ward, or one of the children in our ward; I love them all so much because they are so amazing to me. I'm grateful to serve in this calling. The Lord has truly blessed me. I hope to leave an everlasting impression on these children that they will carry with them throughout their lives. God is so good to me. He is so present in my life. The Gospel is true and I bear testimony that He will deliver and continue to bless. I know that with all my heart. I say this in Jesus' name, Amen.

Chapter 9

KEEPING MY SECOND ESTATE

Verily, Verily, I say unto you, ye are little children, and
ye have not as yet understood how great blessings the
Father hast in his own hands and prepared for you;
And ye cannot bear all things now; nevertheless, be of good
cheer, for I will lead you along. The kingdom is yours and the
blessings thereof are yours, and the riches of eternity are yours.
—Doctrine and Covenants 78:17-18

You may ask, why doesn't God just make life easy and heal me from the disease, or why would He give me the illness anyway? I've heard it all, even that I was cursed or that going on a mission to Fiji caused this illness, etc. The answer to the many wondering questions is that this is the plan. Life and all that it has to offer is part of God's plan for His children. We are all dealt different cards in life, or call it how you will, but we are all born into this life with a body and with the intention to follow God's plan by faith and learning to deal with the trials we will be faced with. I have had many trials, but my hardest trials have also been the ones that taught me so much about myself and about God; how when I involved Him and allowed Him to help me, that is when I was able to endure that trial a lot easier. My faith increased, and my desire to be obedient and follow the examples of the Savior grew stronger.

Yes, God has the power to heal me of this disease, but … if He can use me by bringing many to Him knowing that my own faith won't fail during the process, then why not use me? Besides, God doesn't force anyone to do anything. So, just like Bishop extends callings to the members in the ward to help serve, I do feel that in the pre-mortal life, God extended a calling to me that I said yes to; actually, many callings that I would be able to fulfill at different points of my life. I feel this is true because when I go through these experiences, I feel a confirmation of the Spirit whisper to my heart and soul that I am fulfilling a call. Having Lupus is just one of those many callings.

What we must know and not forget is that in the plan of salvation, we will have trials. That is part of life, part of the plan. That is how we learn to grow and become like God in faith, in patience, in forgiveness, in love, and so on. How we choose to deal with our trials is the test. Though many times we will most likely fail before we become better in what we are trying to be taught by God, we shouldn't feel alone. We shouldn't give up, either. We shouldn't ignore the most powerful source that we have on our side and that is our Savior, Jesus Christ. Use the atonement of Jesus Christ for repentance, healing, strength, comfort, reassurance, and whatever else we are in need of at that moment and time.

Heavenly Father is a loving Father and will not force anything upon anyone. He offers and invites us to come and partake of His love and wants to give us all He has. However, we must accept that invitation by submitting to His will and being obedient.

The devil also offers and invites us to partake of what he disguises as happiness, goodness, or peace. Yet, he has no power or authority other than that which enslaves a soul and traps them into a pit of darkness. I encourage all to look at their current situation, and if the results of their choices aren't leading them down a path of eternal happiness, then it is time to make different choices—and may I add, to include the Lord in those choices.

I am blessed. Having Lupus hasn't been easy, but I have witnessed so many miracles because of it. I've met so many great people that crossed my path because of this illness. I have seen and learned things that I know I wouldn't have seen or learned any other way. So, no, I don't see this as a curse. No, I don't feel like God is punishing me. No, I don't want to be healed if I can continue to help with this work by bearing my testimony to the world about His marvelous love and matchless power.

God loves us and wants us to return to Him. However, we have to want to return to Him and live like Him. When you have tasted the goodness of God, you know there is nothing else comparable to His love, to His goodness. You begin to do all you can and all you're supposed to so that you can have this goodness with you always. Obedience; not compelled or forced obedience, but a willingness to obey is the key.

The Savior was baptized, not because He was a sinner, because He wasn't; but to obey His father in Heaven and to set the example for us. Although we are all in need of baptism to cleanse us from our wrongdoings, it also shows that same obedience that the Lord did when we willingly walk into the waters of baptism and follow the path that our Savior set for us. I love this Gospel. It's perfect. Not the people, but the Gospel itself is perfect. And if we live by it, we can obtain that perfect happiness and that perfect joy no matter what trials come our way. We place our hope and faith in our Father in Heaven who loves us so much. This is not our stop; we are just passing through. In the name of Jesus Christ, Amen!

ABOUT THE AUTHOR

 Originally from Chicago, Keela Jackson resides in Las Vegas, Nevada. She loves spending her time with family, serving others, playing the piano, and writing. She has been a member of the Church of Jesus Christ of Latter Day Saints for twenty years. In 2003, while serving a mission for the church in the Fiji Suva Mission, Keela was diagnosed with Lupus SLE. Despite her physical trials, she continues to stay her positive self and focus on being happy and living out her dreams. A dream that's been dreamt since a little girl, Keela is happy to present to you her first book, An Undying Testimony. This book speaks of her love for the Gospel of Jesus Christ, and how she overcame many of her challenges with having Lupus by leaning on her love for the Savior, and trusting in His love for her.

Printed in the United States
By Bookmasters